D1233661

HQ
767.15
.R83
1996

Rudy, Kathy.

Beyond pro-life and
pro-choice.

$23.00   SEP   1996

DATE			

CHICAGO PUBLIC LIBRARY
MOUNT GREENWOOD BRANCH
DISCARD

BAKER & TAYLOR

BEYOND
PRO-LIFE AND
PRO-CHOICE

BEYOND PRO-LIFE AND PRO-CHOICE

Moral Diversity in the Abortion Debate

—◦—

Kathy Rudy

BEACON PRESS

Boston

Beacon Press
25 Beacon Street
Boston, Massachusetts 02108-2892

Beacon Press books
are published under the auspices of
the Unitarian Universalist Association of Congregations.

© 1996 by Kathy Rudy
All rights reserved
Printed in the United States of America

00 99 98 97 96   8 7 6 5 4 3 2 1

Text design by Janis Owens
Printed on acid-free, recycled paper ♾ ♻

Library of Congress Cataloging-in-Publication Data
can be found on page.

For my teachers

JANE TOMPKINS
STANLEY HAUERWAS
JEAN O'BARR

11010 S.   60655

Contents

-◄o►-

CONTENTS

PART TWO

THE LIMITATIONS OF THE CURRENT DEBATE

Acknowledgments

◄○►

I have accrued many debts in the process of writing this book and wish to acknowledge them here. I am grateful to Duke University for supporting my research on the issue of abortion with grants and scholarships throughout my graduate education. I am also thankful for the Dempster fellowship awarded by the United Methodist Church in my second year of graduate school and a dissertation fellowship from the Louisville Institute for the Study of American Religion in my fourth and final year. I also owe a great debt to my friends at Princeton University's Center for the Study of American Religion; as a postdoctoral fellow there, I both learned new thinking and revised old. I am especially indebted to John Wilson and Bob Wuthnow at Princeton for the spark of new ideas, and to Drew Faust and Charles, Jess, and Staley Rosenberg for their general and unwavering hospitality.

I also want to thank the many friends who have welcomed me back to Duke. I am especially grateful to Randy Styres, Liz Clark, Russ Richey, Tom Ferraro, and Tom Langford, each of whom has read parts of this manuscript and has made a significant contribution to this project. My family, Jan and Kate Radway, provided me with the emotional and financial support one needs to undertake a new career in the middle of life, while our animals—Flannery, Cameron, and Smoky—watched over me as I wrote. I am also grateful to my editor at Beacon, Susan Worst, for her assistance and insights into the project.

Finally, as I look over the pages of this book, I see even more clearly the influence of those teachers who, early on, set for me a rigorous and satisfying intellectual agenda. I owe my greatest debt to Jane Tompkins, Stanley Hauerwas, and Jean O'Barr, for they taught me not only to believe in myself, but more important, to believe in things bigger than myself. I am grateful for the way that each has changed my life, and hope only that I can pass onto others what has been given so generously to me. This book is for them.

AN EARLIER VERSION OF CHAPTER 1 was published in the *Journal of Medical Humanities* 15, no. 4 (1994). Parts of chapter 2 were published as "The Double Effect/Proportionalist Controversy" in a special issue of *South Atlantic Quarterly,* entitled *Catholic Lives/Contemporary Lives* 93, no. 3 (1994). Part of chapter 6 was published as "Thinking through the Ethics of Abortion" in *Theology Today* 15, no. 2 (1994). I am grateful to all these journals for permission to reprint this work.

Introduction

◄○►

You are driving down the highway, thinking of nothing in particular, when you happen upon a billboard that reads, "Abortion Is Murder." Next to these words is a sketchy image that could certainly represent a third-trimester fetus, but could also, without too much imagination, be a newborn baby. Depending on who you are, you may see this image as a fetus about to be aborted, and respond by affirming, "Yes, abortion is murder." Or you may dismiss it as a conservative ploy to misrepresent the degree of development of aborted fetal matter, a ploy that, although meant to invoke compassion, fills you with rage. Or you may view it as something of a misrepresentation, but one that nonetheless makes you think about the deep moral implications of abortion. Or you may react to the billboard any number of other ways; depending on who you are.

In the first part of this book, I will show how the practice of abortion is understood from various contextualized standpoints. The chapters that follow will delineate several different moral views of abortion, views that stem from conflicts between and within various religious and political institutions. These moral views are shaped, reflected, and at times obscured by the language used in the abortion debate. The words "pro-life" or "anti-abortion" may be used to label the same position; the difference lies in the orientation of the speaker.

Some arguments will speak of the products of conception while opposing arguments will address that same subject as an unborn baby or child. One person will see a death where another sees only an exercise of rights. One position will see a pregnant woman where another sees a mother. How we define and describe the subjects and events involved in the act of abortion are intricately connected to our moral evaluation of it. The abortion billboard signifies different meanings for different people because it is read against the landscapes of differing realities.

However, the current abortion debates function as if we all meant the same thing by "abortion." In the media, in schools, and in churches, we speak as if the cultural and linguistic barriers that stand between us at the level of political commitments have nothing to do with the description of abortion itself. We believe that we may have differing opinions regarding the morality of the act, but that we stand in agreement concerning what the act actually is. The emotions attached to the abortion issue may vary, we think, but the assumption that we are all referring to the same act is never questioned. As participants in the abortion debate, we often believe that the issue exists apart from our evaluation of it. I will suggest to the contrary that historical contexts and ethical judgments cannot be suspended when discussing abortion. Rather, such contingencies constitute the meaning of the act. Ethical convictions, I suggest, are not added to "abortion" as a secondary measure but are inextricably combined with the way we understand the issue. We cannot set aside these convictions, even in order to agree on what abortion is, because they are the things that give shape and meaning to the issue itself. By describing abortion as if our moral frameworks did not exist, we neglect the very thing that permits us to see abortion in the first place.

The incoherence associated with the abortion controversy stems from the fact that people are using the term without recognizing that it signals divergent and often conflicting meanings. By speaking of abortion abstractly and without context, we assume that political valences and convictions can be abstracted from some core essence of the act itself. There is, however, no one thing accurately or adequately called "abortion." Abortions only exist in the lives of concrete people in differing cultural locations. These locations, and the various political, religious, and ethical convictions which characterize and accompany them, construct different meanings and definitions for the term abortion. In these often competing locations, people do not all see the same act when viewing an "abortion"; rather they see, as I will demonstrate, different acts, dependent, of course, on who they are and where they are located.

One example from Elizabeth Anscombe's *Intention* is worth quoting at length, as it demonstrates the role of this cultural framing in the determination of meaning and morality.

Let us ask: is there any description which is the description of an action? And let us consider a concrete situation. A man is pumping water into the cistern which supplies drinking water to a house. Someone has found a way of systematically contaminating the source with a deadly cumulative poison whose effects are unnoticeable until they can no longer be cured. The house is regularly inhabited by a small group of party chiefs, with their immediate families, who are in control of a great state; they are engaged in exterminating the Jews and perhaps plan a world war. The man who contaminated the source has calculated that if these people are destroyed some good men will get into power who will govern well, or even institute the Kingdom of Heaven on earth and secure a good life for all the people; and he has revealed his calculation, together with the fact about the poison, to the man who is pumping. The death of the inhabitants of the house will, of course, have all sorts of other effects; e.g., that a number of people unknown to these men will receive legacies, about which they know nothing.

This man's arm is going up and down, up and down. Certain muscles, with Latin names which doctors know, are contracting and relaxing. Certain substances are getting generated in some nerve fibers—substances whose generation in the course of voluntary movements interests physiologists. The moving arm is casting a shadow on a rockery where at one place and from one position it produces a curious effect as if a face were looking out of the rockery. Further, the pump makes a series of clicking noises, which are in fact beating out a noticeable rhythm.

Now we ask: What is this man doing? What is the description of his action?[1]

Anscombe's point is that there is no final or correct description that is independent of interest and context. Even the political implication she describes may not be noticed by the doctor who sees in the movement a new insight regarding the classification of muscles, or by the physiologist who is granted permission to extract the substances from this man's arm for experimental purposes, or by the person who hears this particular rhythm as a code, cadence, or symphony. In each of these contexts, the action potentially produces a different, overriding interpretation. There is no one thing that is really happening. Furthermore, the rudimentary description of "a man pumping water" does not signify what is really happening, any more than any of the other descriptions do. If this man were on trial for the execution of the household, for example, "pumping water" would not at all describe the activity for which he was being tried. The "correct" description is dictated by the logic of the circumstances in which you stand, in short, by the way you see the world.

Let us imagine for a moment that the physiologist and musician from Anscombe's example come into contact later that day. The first might say to the second, "Today I made the most wonderful discovery regarding enzymes produced in exercise," while the second might report, "Today I heard the most beautiful rhythm, which inspired me to write a symphony." These two people may never discover that their respective insights originated in ostensibly the same act. Indeed, if a third person were to suggest that these two people had actually experienced the same act, the two might strongly disagree. Each saw what was most important to him and passed over the aspects that did not make sense or were uninteresting; the physiologist probably did not hear the beat, and the muscles and enzymes never entered the head of the music lover. We see in the world what we are taught to see; we notice and interact with those aspects that we are taught to understand as interesting and worthy of attention.

As Wittgenstein has argued compellingly, "The concept of 'seeing' makes a tangled impression. I look at the landscape, my gaze ranges over it, I see all sorts of distinct and indistinct movement; this impresses itself sharply on me, that is quite hazy." Wittgenstein continues, "And now look at all that can be meant by 'description of what is seen.' . . . There is not one genuine proper case of such description—the rest being vague, something which awaits clarification, or which must be swept aside as rubbish."[2] What we see in the world is dependent upon how we have learned to name things, how we evaluate the importance, and how we are taught to describe the world. There isn't one genuine description, but rather many possible ways of describing. Take, for example, a man who is pumping water that has *not* been poisoned. While his action might very well go completely unnoticed by many of us, he could conceivably spark the interest and attention of the doctor or the physiologist or the musician just as much as Anscombe's man did. The same is true of abortion: it is not the case that we come upon an act of abortion and subsequently interpret it as morally right or wrong. Rather, we only see the act of abortion as a product or result of some ethically evaluative framework or tradition.

Some people might suggest that differences involved in alternative constructions of "abortion" are produced not so much by the description of the event as by the intention of the agent. Anscombe, for example, uses her man pumping water to argue that the nature of an action is constituted by the intention of the person who occasioned the act. In her opinion, the actor's intention must be included in a true and right description. Thus, for a man who was deliberately pumping poisoned water into a house, the correct description of his action must contain the intention of murder. Anything else, for Anscombe, would be misrepresentative. While I am obviously sympathetic to the idea of contextualized description, I am uneasy about placing the weight of emphasis on intention. We cannot, I suggest, count on the fact that everybody will be truthful about all their intentions. Moreover, we are not always able to identify our own intentions. Our self-knowledge, especially in relation to troublesome ethical issues, is often limited.

Our tendency to describe abortion one way rather than another is produced not by our own individual intention but rather by the logics of the systems which make the world intelligible to us. These logics of morality flourish inside each of us. They created us, and their preservation is the point behind our existence. They are engaged in wars of intelligibility; the world of representation is their ammunition and we are simply the sites of their struggle. Although we may be products of more than one logic, when we describe an event or artifact one way rather than another, one of them has won. We are the mechanisms for the survival of these systems, and the issue behind description is not our own intention, but their power.

In each of the communities I examine in the chapters that follow—the medical profession, the Roman Catholic Church, evangelical communities involved in the rescue movement, and various feminist communities (all of which, admittedly, have different voices within them)—different notions of childrearing and family dictate differing levels of tolerance for the procedure known as abortion. In some of the communities, "abortion" is understood as necessary. In others, it is not tolerated. Still in others, it is acceptable only when surrounded by certain prescribed conditions. Often, particular attitudes toward abortion are consciously employed to signify membership in a particular faction of the community. In all of these investigations, I assume that the morality of abortion—that is, whether the community sees it as right or wrong, acceptable or not—is intrinsically related to those things that help construct or contribute to the community's ideology of abortion.[3] By ideology I mean the set of theories and practices used to construct meaning in everyday life.

To understand the complexities involved in the act of describing abortion, I looked at a broad range of sources. In some cases, the writings of Christian theologians and moral philosophers adequately described the meanings of abortion in particular communities. In other cases, however, they seemed out of sync with the way a particular community understood itself in relation to abortion. Consequently, I drew on many nontraditional sources as well, from anthropologies, ethnographies, and histories to videos, trade paperbacks, fiction, "junk mail," and other everyday artifacts of human communities. In each of the contexts I examine, when someone speaks about abortion, I will demonstrate that they mean something specific and very often different than what their neighbors mean when they speak about abortion.

My analysis in part 1 is not intended to be a comprehensive survey of all the possible meanings of abortion constructed within competing communities, or even of all the possible variations within the more complex communities I focus on. While investigations into the morality of abortion from other perspectives—such as that of Jewish, Marxist, black Christian, or mainline Protestant communities—are undoubtedly important to this contextualization process, I do not try to be exhaustive. Rather, it is my hope that we can use these types of analyses to talk more precisely about what competing discourses mean by abortion.

The four chapters in part 1 investigate the methodological frameworks used in four competing communities for determining the morality of abortion; although there are significant variations and exceptions, each of these communities adheres to a recognizable ethical framework. Chapter 1, "The Reproduction of America: Understanding Liberalism's View of Abortion," argues that the use of abortion in the context of new reproductive technologies most closely follows the reason-based ethic associated with classical liberalism. I discuss in this chapter how American medicine increasingly leads to the abortions of "defective fetuses," whose imperfections are themselves discovered as a result of advances in medicine. New reproductive technologies can now scan for more than two hundred genetic and biological defects; the logic attached to these technologies strongly supports the "treatment" of abortion when a defect is found. Indeed, some doctors refuse to perform an amniocentesis unless a woman agrees beforehand to abort if a defect is discovered. In this system, I suggest, these abortions are not a matter of choice, but rather are mandated. In this light, abortions shore up America's liberal profile by eliminating those fetuses that will never be able to reason.

Chapter 2, "The Catholic Construction of Abortion: Double Effect, Proportionalism, and Casuistry," investigates the contours of abortion in various ethical frameworks associated with Roman Catholicism. Here I argue that abortion is illicit throughout Catholicism in part as a result of general theological convictions. That is, all babies, in traditional Catholic thinking, are welcomed and will be provided for by the abundance of God. In a system that believes that there will always be enough to go around, abortion is considered wrong simply because it is unnecessary. This chapter also investigates the growing conflict in Catholic America between traditionalists and proportionalists, a conflict which heightens the differences between competing formulations of moral behavior. As American Catholics struggle to develop their own moral theology distinct from that of the Vatican, the use and acceptance of abortion changes dramatically, creating still another construction of the morality of abortion.

Chapter 3, " The Function of Abortion in the Rescue Movement," studies the Bible-based ethic of the evangelical subculture of Operation Rescue, the movement that attempts to close abortion clinics by holding protest demonstrations in front of specific target clinics. In this chapter, I suggest that Operation Rescue encompasses different ways of being opposed to abortion, indeed different ways of rescuing, and that those differences signify complex memberships in groups that, save for that opposition, hold little else in common. Although the theology associated with New Right televangelists Pat Robertson and Jerry Falwell appears to define Operation Rescue, a deeper investigation of its ideology indicates that many rescuers hold much more progressive religious and social views. In this context, a believer's view of the legal, moral, and spiritual nature of abortion is linked to her location in a broad spectrum of Christian activism.

Finally, chapter 4, "Conflicted over Men, Women, and Sex: Abortion in the Frame of Contemporary Feminisms," investigates the attitudes and arguments feminists have marshaled over the last three decades regarding abortion. From radical "pro-abortionists" to cultural feminists, from pro-sex feminists to liberal "pro-choicers," women who have been involved in the contemporary feminist movement have done so for many reasons. I argue in this chapter that "feminism" is actually a collection of competing positions and attitudes which hold women as a central category of analysis but resolve the problem of women's oppression in a variety of ways; nowhere is this more apparent than in the issues surrounding abortion. I am especially interested in the history and development of the "pro-choice" faction of feminism, which bases its ethical methodology on a rights-based methodology. My work suggests that feminists are positioned differently on the issue of abortion in relation to different ways of interpreting the problem of oppression and, relatedly, different ways of bringing about liberation.

My decision to study these particular communities emerged in part from my own history. Novelist Lee Smith has written that "a writer cannot pick her material any more than she can pick her parents; her material is given to her by the circumstances of her birth, by how she first hears language." The first half of this book witnesses to the truth of this statement. Raised as a Roman Catholic in America, I recited the Nicene Creed and pledged allegiance to the U.S. flag every morning in my parish school, starting each day with a reminder of the conflicts that the church and the state had both agreed to ignore. My uncles, in the name of democracy, killed other Christians and died in wars that our parish priests supported. While the church taught us that our religious convictions must be primary, the world of television and mass communication taught us that our lives were made possible by the ideology of America. Consequently, distinctions between "secular" and "religious" were few; Thanksgiving, Christmas, Easter, and July Fourth all honored our debts to the Pilgrims, Jesus, and George Washington. By the time I reached adulthood, I tried to opt out of such uncomfortable conflicts by leaving Catholicism and joining the United Methodist Church. My membership remains in the UMC, a more comfortable convergence for me, for better or worse, of Americanism and Christianity.

My aim in these first four chapters is to suggest that when we talk about "abortion," we are often actually talking about different things, that the meanings, associations, and contexts of "abortion" differ from community to community. In the current conflict over abortion, attitudes are organized into two positions: pro-life and pro-choice. In the logic of today's debate, there is no room for third or fourth alternatives; each side claims a zero-sum game, an either/or structure. This bifurcation suggests, for example, that Catholic and evangelical opposition to abortion are morally identical. Similarly, the assumption is made that all pro-choicers hold morally analogous commitments; no distinction need be made between people who endorse or accept abortion for different reasons, or between those who support abortion in every case and those who support it only under certain conditions. The distinction between pro-life and pro-choice preempts and obstructs conversations about what we're talking about when we talk about abortion. When all the possible positions are reduced to two common denominators, the details that give these contexts both political substance and moral character are lost. In these first four chapters, I try to reveal the moral richness involved in competing constructions of abortion.

THE SECOND PART OF THIS BOOK, "The Limitations of the Current Debate," offers concrete criticisms of the current pro-life/pro-choice argument from three related perspectives. It is not only the case that the bifurcated discourse distorts and misrepresents the ways that most people relate to the issue of abortion; it also serves to truncate and restrict the deeper commitments of communities involved in the debate. That is, because feminism and Christianity are forced to fit into the pro-choice/pro-life frame that has been imposed on them, neither community can utilize its full range of resources or strive for its own particular vision of the good life in relation to abortion. Whereas the first half of this book displays how the abortion debates are simply inadequate, the second half suggests ways that they are in fact detrimental.

Chapter 5, "The Uneasy Marriage between Feminism and 'Pro-Choice,'" argues against the narrowly defined, liberal-based pro-choice campaign and in favor of a wider-ranging "reproductive rights" strategy. I suggest that in organizing people on the ground of keeping abortion legal, the ideology of pro-choice does a disservice to a great number of women who cannot afford abortions even if they are legal, or conversely, who cannot marshal the necessary economic or social resources to carry a pregnancy to term. More broadly, I argue in this chapter that the same liberal philosophy which mandates the abortion of defective fetuses very often inadvertently discriminates against childbearers. What we need is a new social theory whereby people are seen not as individuated, competing subjects, but rather as part of a larger community, a community which can support a woman not only with the legal "right" to an abortion, but with the material resources should she choose not to abort.

Chapter 6, "Christianity and the Abortion Wars," examines the limitations that the pro-life/pro-choice dichotomy places on the work of the church. Because many Christians are divided over the abstract principles of when life begins and whose rights are at stake, the church is largely unable to function as a community of caring, called believers. This chapter advocates a new methodology that will allow Christians to transcend the chasm created by the contemporary secular conflict; in basing our abortion ethics on the historical practice known as casuistry, I suggest we can respond more faithfully to the moral dilemma of abortion today.

Just as part 1 was based on my own autobiographical location and dictated by the communities that have formed me, so chapters 5 and 6 are informed by the vision and hope I continue to find within both feminism and Christianity. As a feminist, I often experience pro-choice argumentation as limited by heterosexist privilege and white, middle-class bias. Although I believe that every woman ought to be able to control her own body, a sole focus on this belief distorts a larger feminist vision wherein women have access to much more than a "right to choose." As a feminist, I believe we need to be working toward ways that break down the racial, class, and heterosexist barriers that exist between women in order to move into a world where women have a greater number of options than pregnancy or abortion. The pro-choice movement, for me, limits that larger vision. Similarly, as a Christian, I see the church as a place which could transcend the pro-life/pro-choice debate, where the lives of female parishioners could take primacy over the abstract commitment to a philosophical principle. Our churches today, however, often seem more committed to court rulings than caring for the disenfranchised. I believe that our tradition calls us to a deeper understanding of community on the issue of abortion.

In the midst of all the fragmentation on the issue of abortion, both Christianity and feminism sustain me; chapters 5 and 6 articulate the understandings that these traditions offer in relation to reproduction and abortion. In this sense, then, these chapters are less descriptive and more prescriptive; they represent my moral arguments about both feminism and Christianity on the issue of abortion, and my vision of where these communities should go in the future. Within both feminism and Christianity, I suggest that there are ways to adjudicate opinions and beliefs about abortion. Although they do not fit into the pro-choice/pro-life frame, the moral guideposts I find in each of these traditions can be used to map new moralities for abortion politics. These two chapters represent my attempts to do so, both as a feminist and as a Christian.

These new mappings of abortion, however, cannot be executed outside the auspices of a particular community; they cannot exist in some imaginary objective space that all communities would agree on. For this reason, chapter 7, "Subjectivity, Fragmentation, and the

Law: An Argument for Repeal," suggests that the most effective way for all traditions to combat the dichotomous pro-choice/pro-life thinking regarding subjectivity and abortion is to advocate repeal of all abortion laws. Only in an environment in which communities are free to display entire lifestyles and everyday practices can ethical commitments regarding things like abortion become clear. In shifting the focus from the legal question, traditions can then expend their energy converting more people, and partially converting others, to their convictions regarding abortion. In so doing, the abortion conflict will no longer be constituted in relation to the legal status of abortion; it will no longer be dominated by "pro-life" or "pro-choice" ideologies. Instead, we will have many different groups expressing different opinions about the value of fetal life, the value of women's lives, the nature of sexuality, and the needs of children. These new dialogues will not necessarily resolve the abortion wars; rather they will give us clearer ideas about what precisely is at stake in the convictions of various competing communities.

Moreover, I argue in the last chapter that any one of us can be constituted at different times and in different circumstances by any number of these communities; people can "see" the morality of abortion differently at different points. Simultaneous membership in competing communities is not only possible, but likely. The American legal system, however, is predicated on a human subject that is theoretically consistent over time and space; it can only account for a subject that is stably positioned in relation to abortion. In this concluding chapter, I suggest that the abortion wars are waged primarily because the law can only conceptualize whole, unified subjects. I argue that a fetus either is viewed as a full subject that has the right not to be aborted or it is viewed not as a subject, in the face of a woman's right to control her reproductive capacities. Because no other possibilities for envisioning human life exist, we are caught in an irresolvable war between pro-choice and pro-life. Thus, it is this fictional concept of the legal, righted subject as unified and undividable that has caused the current abortion conflict. "Women's rights" are pitted against the "rights of the unborn" because—within the liberal system of American law—we have no other way of conceiving human beings than as fully coherent individuals who need protection from one another. Because we only see people in whole "individuated" units, we have no way to discuss the ambiguous nature of the developing fetus.

In a sense, my thinking in this final chapter is a result of my own fragmented biography, especially in relation to the issue of abortion. Because I have been formed by various competing ideologies, I often experience the issue in a conflicted manner. I can't seem to locate myself firmly on one side of the divide or the other, as both sides seem far too limited in their articulation of the larger social good. When I look past the divide into the more complicated terrain of many competing ideologies, I see myself reflected in a number of places; I see value in the social good of many of the traditions and ideologies that have formed me. This book attempts to draw out the best aspects of these traditions—like the fact that Catholics welcome children, or that feminists believe that women should be able to determine what happens to their bodies, or that evangelicals believe that religious convictions have more than "private" significance.

In order to see the good involved in all of these traditions simultaneously, two things must happen. First, we must surrender and transcend the notion that the abortion debate is constituted by two sides. It's not. Categorizing people into one of these two camps simply obscures the larger worldviews which drive specific communities to have opinions about such ethical matters. Second, I believe we also have to give up the idea that every single one of us exists in only one community or within one ideology. This is the fiction that grounds

American law and divides us into the mutually exclusive categories of "pro-choice" and "pro-life."

The fragmentation exists not only on a personal and philosophical level, but also on a larger social level. I suggest in my last chapter that we ought to view ourselves, as well as pregnant mothers, fetuses, and society itself, as fragmentary instead of unitary. For those convinced that the American legal system is the most appropriate pathway for social change, the argument for repeal contained in this chapter may seem senseless. However, I wish here to challenge the foundation upon which the law—and most of our thinking—is built, to contest the effectiveness of liberal subjectivity in describing the realities of our fragmented lives in relation to abortion. I do not attempt here to work within the contemporary legal system but to push forward to a different way of seeing morality, based not on unitary subjectivity but on the harvesting of positive aspects of competing ideologies. Only by moving away from legally based debates and opinions can we begin to solve some of the problems associated with abortion.

Abortion is only one word. But this one word has many meanings. Although it almost always invokes some framework, we cannot tell, beforehand, which framework the word will activate: "The confusions which occupy us arise when language is like an engine idling, not when it is doing work."[4] "Abortion" is an idling engine. It is not doing any work; it is not signifying an intelligible moral act. Rather, it stands as a placeholder for a collection of acts that, as I shall demonstrate, are not at all morally equivalent.

Moreover, because we may hold memberships in conflicting communities, we ourselves see abortion (and our social memberships) in conflicting, fragmented patterns. I tell the stories of the communities that have formed me and continue to influence me on the issue of abortion as a way of inviting readers to think about what they believe about the morality of abortion and why. If we all begin by scratching below the (admittedly durable) surface of pro-choice versus pro-life rhetoric, I believe we will find fascinating, intricate, and even attractive worldviews supporting our abortion ethics. Only by telling the stories found there—and allowing others to participate in our worlds—will we ever be able to solve the conflicts associated with abortion.

PART ONE

MAPPING THE MORALITIES OF ABORTION

CHAPTER ONE

The Reproduction of America

Understanding Liberalism's View of Abortion

—◄○►—

*It was so hard for me to get an abortion, since I had been so
excited about the pregnancy and very much wanted to be a
mother. But when the amniocentesis showed that I would have
a Down's syndrome baby, I knew I wasn't prepared either
emotionally or financially to raise a child who is likely to have
serious physical and mental problems.*

The Boston's Women's Health Book Collective
The New Our Bodies, Ourselves

By 1770, Immanuel Kant had begun the writing of his *Critique
of Pure Reason,* a work that attempted to demarcate the vast-
ness of the cognitive powers of reason and the subsequent freedom
that the sole use of reason entailed. Kant's desire to articulate human
capacity for pure rationality propelled the discipline of philosophy
into an era characterized by assertions that human beings were independent and self-reliant. These late-eighteenth-century ideas produced by Kant, Locke, Hobbes, Rousseau, and others were brought
across the Atlantic to germinate the nascent political ideology of the
newly forming United States of America.

By 1776, the time of the writing of the Declaration of Independence, the principles of rationality had captured the heart of America. The Christian "City on the Hill" envisioned by Puritanism had

given way, on levels of public discourse at least, to a government founded upon the self-evidence of human rights. Being American meant being free not only from Britain, but from restraints that confined identity to a particular religion or sovereign. These freedoms were bought by the recognition of every individual's natural capacity for reason and self-sufficiency.

In the abortion debate, the logic of liberalism is best illustrated through a discussion of new reproductive technologies. I draw connections here between the medical procedures produced by such technologies, most specifically the use of prenatal tests which result in abortion, and the dictates of American liberal theory. There is, I believe, a strong link between certain contemporary American abortion practices and American liberalism's formulation of and emphasis on rational, unified individualism. The criterion of reason as the sole measure of humanity has influenced the conditions under which we reproduce and, consequently, under which we abort. Although America purports to offer certain kinds of freedom to all individuals, only those who exercise the capacity for rationality are in fact permitted to reap the benefits of liberal society.

Having made such a bald statement, I must qualify what I mean. I do not believe that Americans willfully and happily choose to abort fetuses that are diagnosed as disabled, abnormal, or nonrational; Americans, for the most part, have compassionate attitudes toward children with disabilities. Rather, physically and mentally disabled fetuses are aborted at increasing rates because the contained and isolated nuclear American family is often unable to organize the social and economic resources necessary to sustain this life. It is not always the case that disabled children are unwanted as a sole result of the disability. Instead, the decision to abort often stems from the fact that extended and alternative family configurations that could help absorb the needs of a disabled child are unavailable. The convictions embedded in the way we structure our lives, I believe, reflect a system that demands that every member of every family be self-sufficient and mentally present, convictions which in turn often require the abortions of fetuses that cannot meet those requirements. Our economy is structured to support our philosophical presuppositions; when economic resources are scarce, those who don't quite fit the larger ideology are the first to be eliminated.

Anthropologist Rayna Rapp expresses the difficulties that accompany choosing to have a disabled child in today's culture. It is worth letting her tell the story herself, as her narrative is based not on academic observation, but rather on the realities she was forced to confront in her own life.

> We were eager to have a child, and prepared to change our lives to make emotional, social, and economic resources available. But the realities of raising a child who could never grow to independence would call forth more than we could muster, unless one or both of us gave up our work, our political commitments, our social existence beyond the household. . . . To keep a Down syndrome child alive through potentially lethal health problems is an act of love with weighty consequences. As we ourselves age, to whom would we leave the person [the fetus] would become? Neither Mike nor I have any living kin who are likely to be young enough, or close enough, to take on this burden after our deaths.[1]

At one time in history, the potential parents might have called on a large, extended family for support. As relatives moved in and out, those who were too old to work outside the home often provided the extra help and supervision necessary to raise a disabled child.[2] In the ideological matrix of the contemporary nuclear family, however, privacy and greater economic control over material conditions are valued to such an extent that few family resources can be devoted either to the inclusion of extended family members or to the care of permanently dependent individuals. Moreover, the state offers families with disabled children minimal assistance because, as I will demonstrate, it is in the state's best financial and ideological interests to allow only healthy babies to be born.

In this chapter, then, I focus only on those abortions produced by prenatal tests which indicate mental or physical abnormalities. Although in China and India, prenatal diagnoses are often used for sex selection, in America these technologies have been used primarily for the detection and subsequent abortion of fetuses with mental and physical impairment.[3] In America, we obtain "perfect" babies (of either sex) through medical procedures which furnish increasingly accurate methods of determining physical and mental characteristics, as well as certain diseases and abnormalities before birth. Technologies such as amniocentesis, chorionic villi sampling, and fetal sonography monitor the health and genetic constitution of the fetus at various stages of development, and as William Arney has suggested, operate as surveillance on the reproduction of humanity.[4] In short, they screen the future population for abnormalities and mandate the abortions of "undesirables" at increasing rates. The discourse of medicine is produced within American liberalism and returns the favor, so to speak, by constructing technologies that reproduce, both in flesh and in spirit, American liberalism. When so much emphasis is placed on rationality, the consequences for those individuals who, in traditional terms, cannot reason are grave.

As Americans seeking clear thinking about abortion, we often limit our discussion only to its legality. This discussion, while important, is of little value in understanding why women might or might not *want* to procure abortions. No woman has an abortion simply because her government declares that she is legally permitted to do so. Similarly, women who choose to carry their babies full term usually do so because they want that baby, not because they believe that that fetus is endowed with an inherent "right" to life. By directing our attention solely to the legality of abortion, we fail to understand what produces our desires to have or not to have abortions, or children, in the first place. Nevertheless, one aspect and product of our relation to rationality is that we attempt to reproduce an America populated by individuals who perpetuate reason-based ideology. That is, who we have sex with, who we bear and raise, and when we abort are not disinterested decisions articulated by entirely free agents. Although liberalism advertises a relatively unconfined freedom in the private sphere, I suggest that allegedly private decisions regarding reproduction are regulated by ideological grammars that lie beyond the limits of consciousness. In many instances of reproduction, there appears to be no choice involved because the logic of the American liberal tradition has made the choice for us.

JOHN RAWLS IS BY CONSENSUS the preeminent contemporary theorist of liberalism, and he provides the clearest schematic formulation of an amorphous body of beliefs operating in American culture. In *A Theory of Justice,* Rawls sets forth what he calls an "original position," that is, an imaginary or hypothetical situation in which individuals choose the principles of a just society without advance knowledge of their own position and circumstances within that society. As Rawls describes it, "The principles of justice are chosen behind a veil of ignorance. This ensures that no one is advantaged or disadvantaged in the choice of principles by the outcome of natural chance or the contingency of social circumstances."[5] This theory is based on the idea that agreement between people must stem not from particularized or parochial beliefs or customs, but rather from reasoned, public consent; the parameters of a just society are set, according to Rawls, by understanding the degree of freedom and protection that we would choose for ourselves and then mapping such a choice onto the rights and duties of all members. The solutions to conflict and to discordant situations cannot rest on attitudes, opinions, convictions, or beliefs, but must be arrived at solely by this rational thought process. In basing these negotiations solely in the realm of reason, justice and fairness to all members will follow.

In his writings since *A Theory of Justice,* Rawls's formulations have taken a decidedly pragmatic turn. In contradistinction to Kant, who located reason in the metaphysical realm, Rawls asserts that reason is located not inside human nature, but rather "within the practical social task of seeking a practicable and working understanding on first principles of justice."[6] That is, it is not the case that humans are born with the reason that leads to justice and fairness in the public sphere; rather, such reason emerges from "common sense" and the "basic intuitive ideas" embedded in the political institutions and traditions of the modern democratic state.[7] In short, Rawls argues that his notion of justice as fairness in the public sphere is a political, not a metaphysical concept.[8]

Thus, according to Rawls, the rationality that makes a being fully human and, consequently, that signifies full membership in liberal society must be learned. Human beings are born only with the capacity to reason; proper moral development must follow in order to initiate any individual fully into the rational, liberal order. Rawls identifies the family as the training ground for the proper development of the sensibilities and emotions that lead to the desire for justice and fairness. As he describes, "The parents must love the child and be worthy objects of his [*sic*] admiration. In this way they arouse in him a sense of his own value and the desire to become the sort of person they are."[9] The values taught in the family nourish the skills needed to negotiate the space of the original position. The family teaches us sympathy, kindness, and compassion for others, which individuals then translate into justice in public discourse. The family, then, enables individuals to take their places in public order.

However, I believe that it is not only the case that families help create public order; the reverse is also true. American political and social order influences the shape of the typical American family. The training that is needed for every American to take up his or her position in public life cannot be provided by *any* sort of family; rather, the American family must be produced by and reproduce a collection of values, commitments, and ideologies which resonate with and reflect the attributes necessary for liberal order. Once we recognize that we are not just families but "American families"—families whose function it is to train young members to negotiate adequately in the original position—we can understand contemporary medical practices associated with reproduction from a new perspective.

In the America of the late twentieth century, the anxieties produced by economic instability and climbing costs of living prohibit many couples from having more than one or two children, or in some cases, from having any children at all. When young families do decide to share their lives, space, and money with offspring, they often feel that they cannot afford, either financially or emotionally, to produce a child that is less than perfect. As a result of these restrictions, the ideal of the perfect child has become the norm for reproduction in America today. It is this ideal that underwrites medicine's fascination with reproductive technologies.[10]

On one level, the race for reproductive technology has been dominated by the impulse to develop interventions which will allow us to conceive our "own" children. In vitro fertilization, artificial insemination by husband or donor, surrogacy, and gametic intrafallopian transfer (GIFT) have now made many types of infertility treatable. As technologies that provide the means for overcoming infertility become increasingly available, American families increasingly exercise the right to copy their own best possible genetic blueprint (their own rationality) in their children.

These same technologies also enable us to conceive children who are, genetically speaking, improvements upon ourselves. That is, the quest for the most perfect child that technology can produce has even extended beyond the logic of the genetically nuclear family. Artificial insemination by donor and GIFT make the chromosomal blueprints of, for example, Nobel prize winners and sports heroes available to all who can afford the price. These technologies have allowed us to articulate more fully the kind of individual who thrives in and reproduces American culture. These children are born into familial ideologies underpinned by the understanding that their chromosomes "cost" the family upwards of as much as $50,000. Although no studies have yet been done of children produced by these reproductive technologies, it seems likely that hi-tech children will think of themselves as "special," as having inside themselves all they will ever need to attain success. Conversely, these children will also learn that, genetically speaking, they have only themselves to blame for their failures. These are precisely the attitudes that render success in the original position. In other words, modern reproductive technologies are inadvertently engineering a more rational and individualized nation; the children produced by such procedures are thought to be better equipped to populate the original position, and consequently to reproduce the conditions of reason by which they were raised.

Although the costs of artificial reproductive techniques are high (the average for one in vitro fertilization, for example, is $30,000), this money is considered well spent in the current cultural ethos of America.[11] Not only will the resulting child more likely possess the desired credentials of rationality, the family will also be understood by the dominant cultural logic as more prosperous. Utilizing these reproductive technologies indicates a good (and in all likelihood costly) medical plan and a high level of disposable income, both of which signify success within the American dream. With these technologies, reproducers not only buy a "perfect" baby but also buy into a higher level of status in American society.

New developments in reproductive technologies assist in the quest for the perfect baby not only by genetically creating "better" children but also by detecting and eliminating fetuses deemed abnormal and defective. In a world where babies are bred for desired characteristics, having a healthy, normal baby becomes nothing less than a duty. While it may appear that medicine simply offers procedures such as diagnostic ultrasound, fetal electrocardiography, and amniocentesis as options for those who desire them, the fear of producing a child that falls outside the boundary of "normal" compels many women to seek premonitory information regarding the status of their fetus. As one of Rayna Rapp's interviewees explained regarding her tests, "If he was gonna be slow, if he wasn't gonna have a shot at being President, that's not the baby we wanted."[12] The bodies and minds of children born with disabilities often serve to demarcate those who are not full participants in American ideology from those who are. By contrast, the consumption of these technologies is not simply a matter of private choice but a necessary indication of full integration into American life.

Reproductive technologies that began with the dream of producing healthier babies have now turned into a nightmare of need and obligation. As Daniel Callahan once wrote of transplantation technology, "No one thought, a century ago, that a person suffering from heart disease 'needed' a heart transplant; death was simply accepted. But the advent of heart transplants was stimulated first by hope, and that hope became concrete need as transplantation succeeded."[13] The same is true, I believe, for prenatal testing. Our desire to produce "normal" children, coupled with the growing achievements of technology, render these tests, in the current cultural logic, necessary. As sociologist Barbara Katz Rothman suggests:

> It is not uncommon to hear women say that they would never have dared a pregnancy at their age without the availability of amniocentesis. I have heard that from women in their early 30s on up. It may very well be true for these women, as things now stand. Pregnancy is just too risky for them to attempt without amniocentesis. But when we talk to women now in their 50s and 60s and older about the children they bore while in their 30s and 40s, they do not talk about fear of Down's Syndrome haunting these pregnancies. That is not to say that they were not indeed at some risk. I am only saying that the risk was not being brought to their attention, and even if they were aware of the risk, they were not focused on it.[14]

Women over thirty (and this age keeps getting lower) often desperately "need"—in Callahan's sense—these tests. The problem with this specific technology, however, is that while we feel we need these tests, we simultaneously and equally fear their results.

Although statistics are not available regarding how many women currently undergo routine prenatal testing, most sources suggest that the number increases yearly. When an anomaly is found, "the decision to abort is most common."[15] More important even than the number of abortions that take place for this reason is the ideology that dictates that these abortions are socially acceptable in today's elitist American context. "In the United States," asserts Rothman, "more than 80 percent of people approve of the use of abortion . . . to prevent the birth of a handicapped or disabled child."[16]

The "acceptability" of these abortions serves to support and perpetuate the apparatus of American liberal theory. That is, Rawlsian liberalism is predicated upon the rationality of every individual; those who run the risk of life without reason are increasingly unwelcome within the logic of the culture in which we live. As Rothman argues, "The genetic counseling, the screening and testing of fetuses, serves the function of 'quality control' on the assembly line of the products of conception, separating out those products we wish to develop from those we wish to discontinue."[17] The "products we wish to discontinue," I believe, are those that cannot easily adapt themselves to liberal logic.

For the women who receive the tests that monitor the health and genetic characteristics of their unborn, little can be done to correct most abnormalities and disabilities in utero. Or, stated more accurately, abortion is the sole method of "treatment" for defective fetuses. Although scientific "breakthroughs" regarding fetal "gene therapy" are sometimes reported in popular media, "we need to be very clear," as Ruth Schwartz Cowan claims, "about what therapy is currently available for most diseases or disabilities that can be diagnosed prenatally: none. The only recourse for patients whose fetuses are diagnosed as having Down's syndrome, or spina bifida, or Turner's syndrome, or Tay-Sachs disease, or sickle cell anemia, or one of the thalassemias is abortion."[18]

Prenatal tests, and the normal fetuses that "pass" these tests, are certainly signifiers of American success. In this logic, then, "failed," "abnormal" fetuses must be aborted if success is sought. That is, in America today, the abortion of the defective fetuses detected by these tests is virtually mandatory. Indeed, as William Arney points out, "[s]ome doctors refuse to do amniocenteses unless the woman is willing to commit herself, *before the test is done*, to an abortion in case a defective fetus is found."[19] These abortions are not freely elected or chosen by anyone, but rather are ultimately part of a system that grants primacy to rationality, health, and normalcy. The products of conception are monitored for their potential ability to someday occupy the original position. Our current technologies set the standards for inspecting these products; as a result, we become the workers whose job it is to reject those fetuses of questionable quality. As biologist Ruth Hubbard writes, "Physicians and scientists need merely provide the techniques that make individual women, and parents, responsible for implementing the society's prejudices, so to speak, by choice."[20]

Throughout its history, American leaders have time and again shown concern with the genetic constitution of the country's population; attempts to purify the gene pool are no new phenomenon. The first attempt occurred at the turn of this century, as some thirty states enacted restrictive marriage laws for mentally deficient people. When this method for limiting the reproduction of mentally handicapped Americans failed, the government allowed states to institute mandatory sterilization laws, many of which are still on the books and greatly contested today.[21] The major problem with these attempts, and the chief reason they failed is that they required the U.S. government to blatantly intervene in the protected private lives of Americans. What the ideology called for, then, was a way to control the gene pool without public intervention in the private realm, a way to help its citizens voluntarily control their genetic future. Amniocentesis and other prenatal tests answered just such a call.

This tacit control of future gene pools has met with significant resistances, especially among those who work against discrimination of the handicapped. Many of these activists strongly suggest that women who are considering abortion as a result of fetal disability should meet and talk with adult disabled people or parents of disabled children.[22] Disability rights activists Susan Wendell and Marsha Saxton both suggest that the cultural stigmas attached to disabled persons occur mostly because we fear such a state of dependency for ourselves.[23] Other writers contest degrading interpretations of disability by narrating their own journeys or by relaying the joys that relationships with disabled children have produced for them.[24] Still others suggest that abortion for reasons of disability be more strongly discouraged, or even criminalized. As one disabled activist argues, "abortion on the grounds of handicap denies us an identity as equal human beings worthy of respect, and calls into question the place in society of disabled individuals."[25]

Disability activists writing from a feminist perspective, however, both support positive views of disability and advocate a woman's right to abortion. As Michelle Fine and Adrienne Asch articulate in their influential "Shared Dreams: A Left Perspective on Disability Rights and Reproductive Rights," "While a fetus resides within her, a woman has the right to decide about her body and her life and to terminate a pregnancy for [disability] or any other reason."[26] According to Fine and Asch, the movement to better the lives of disabled persons should not interfere with a woman's right to control her body. While these feminists work to resist oppressive interpretations of disability by advocating increased education and awareness, they also suggest that denying women access to abortion would jeopardize women's rights and freedom. Resistance to negative interpretations of disability should not, they argue, place disproportionate social and economic burdens on women, which would certainly occur if a woman's right to abortion were restricted for any reason. Although I stand in full agreement regarding this last point, I believe we must also investigate the ways that American medicine and American liberalism benefit from these particular abortions.

Ruth Hubbard has drawn a connection between contemporary abortion of disabled fetuses and the eugenic policies of Nazi Germany. What became the racial hygiene programs of the Third Reich were not, Hubbard notes, initially directed against "Jews, Gypsies,

Gays, and eastern Europeans, the kinds of people who come to mind when we think of the Nazi persecution and extermination programs. That came later. Initially, racial hygiene was designed to eliminate 'hereditary pathology' [i.e., the disabled]."[27] When she proceeds to compare American cultural history with that of Nazi Germany, Hubbard makes the troubling point that any defense of the right to abort disabled American fetuses could be construed as an inadvertent eugenic policy. The current justifications of abortion carry out the logic of nationalistic programs not far removed from the one used in Nazi Germany to legitimate the purification of the race.

Obstetric technologies can now test for nonfatal fetal disorders, as well as for diseases that will not surface until later in life. Biologists report that most of us carry three to five abnormal recessive genes that could surface in future generations.[28] The line between rationality and retardation, between perfect and defective, is becoming less and less clear. Because this American drive toward perfection continues to expand, questions about who shall live, and who shall receive those scarce medical resources, are on the minds of most ethicists and health care professionals today. And it is in the solutions to these moral quandaries that liberalism's commitment to rationality can be most readily detected.

For example, H. Tristram Engelhardt, one of today's most prominent medical ethicists, claims that the only appropriate approach to such dilemmas is to understand morality as having two levels. Basing his ideas on the assumption that the fundamental ethical task of a pluralistic society is to solve moral dilemmas without violence, Engelhardt claims that our primary moral commitment must be to the "peaceable community."[29] Interaction in the public realm of the peaceable community, he argues, operates on a contentless and context-free set of principles that ensure every individual his or her right to freedom in private matters, matters that do not affect others. A second level of moral adherence may take place in the private sphere, where, according to Engelhardt, individuals may subscribe to the particularities of religions or cultural opinions. However, commitments to these local moralities must never take primacy over the peaceable community; we must never care about some aspect contained by the private sphere in a way that conflicts with our primary commitment to live peacefully with individuals of different persuasions. Thus, in Engelhardt's thinking, the peaceable community does not constitute a tradition, but rather offers a way of suspending or reaching across traditions by virtue of reason.[30] Only those who reason, he suggests, will be able to maintain a solid commitment to the overarching peaceable community; those who are mentally handicapped might confuse the two levels of commitment and therefore challenge the entire system.

In a similar fashion, philosopher Richard Rorty suggests a category common to all beings, one that he calls "human solidarity." Rorty suggests that solidarity doesn't allow us to clear away prejudices, but rather invites us to overcome them. As he illustrates it, "If you were a Jew in the period when the trains were running to Auschwitz, your chances of being hidden by your gentile neighbors were greater if you lived in Denmark or Italy than if you lived in Belgium. A common way of describing this difference is by saying that many Danes and Italians showed a greater sense of human solidarity which many Belgians lacked."[31] The ability to respond to what is human in our neighbors constitutes, for Rorty, the core of liberal morality: "The traditional philosophical way of spelling out what we mean by 'human solidarity' is to say that there is something within each of us—our essential humanity—which resonates to the presence of this same thing in other human beings."[32]

Although Rorty believes that the liberal grounding of morality in inherent reason is philosophically mistaken, in his view liberalism is nevertheless the moral tradition that most of us have inherited. Rorty's categories of "irony" and "contingency" attempt to strip liberal theory of its metaphysical ontology and constitute the postmodern or antifoundational facet of his work. While his disassociation from traditional rational foundations is philosophically persuasive, his privileging of an essential humanness over and against particularized moral commitments simply reconfigures, at least on the practical level, the concepts set forth by Rawls. Put differently, although Rorty suggests that "[t]he social glue holding together the ideal liberal society . . . consists in little more than a consensus that the point of social organization is to let everybody have a chance at self-creation to the best of his or her abilities," he overlooks the problem that, in America today, precisely what constitutes a "self" with the potential for self-creation is often predetermined by current reproductive technologies.[33]

Engelhardt promotes an understanding of self and personhood that is, however, frighteningly clear. He suggests that full medical care is primarily intended for "persons in the strict sense of moral agents, which includes patients who discuss their problems with their physicians and come to agreements about treatment." He thus makes the distinction between "person" and "human" by suggesting that persons "show evidence of being rational," while "[t]his is not the case in the instance of infants, the profoundly mentally retarded, and other individuals who cannot determine for themselves their own hierarchy of costs and benefits." According to Engelhardt, "such entities are not persons in any strict sense" and, although human, cannot demand the same level of medical care as reasoned "persons" can.[34]

In Engelhardt's view, only rational persons compose the peaceable community, display human solidarity, or populate the original position, and therefore only rational persons should reap the benefits of full medical care and freedom in the private realm offered by liberal society. As he argues, "persons have a right, unless they have agreed otherwise, to act at liberty as long as they are not employing unconsented-to force against other innocent persons, or imposing unjustifiable suffering on innocent organisms." Engelhardt concludes from this premise that "parents who judge that a defective newborn should either be allowed painlessly to die or be aided in dying painlessly offend against neither of these two constraints." Allowing/causing the death of disabled newborns is completely in keeping with the logic proposed by a system that distinguishes persons from humans, for "[t]o force parents [persons] to treat a severely defective newborn [human] may indeed count as imposing by force and without justification a particular view of beneficence."[35] Allowing/causing the death of disabled newborns also, I think, helps to make abortion of defective fetuses appear as the superior ethical choice.

The rationale that separates persons from humans is so clear to Engelhardt that he suggests that the abortion of normal fetuses is in fact not an ethical problem at all: "Despite its capacity to attract major public interest and sustain bitter public debate, abortion is not a serious moral issue. It is not possible to justify, in general secular terms, holding embryos and fetuses to be persons."[36] In Engelhardt's system, then, the abortion of defective fetuses is justified on two counts: first, because any fetus is, by definition, not yet a person, and second because a fetus with a disability will most likely never develop into a person. Such a position renders these abortions virtually inevitable.

American liberalism is part of and reinforced by the decisions that pregnant women make about their bodies, their resources, and their families. Even when a woman wants to continue the pregnancy of a mentally or physically disabled fetus, her commitments to her existing family and community often prompt her to choose otherwise. One woman who chose to abort a defective fetus despite the fact that she works professionally with the severely and profoundly retarded, did so because, as Rothman explains, "it was not what she knew about the fetus that determined the decision, but what she knew about the world." As this woman herself articulates it:

> If all of society—including extended family—shared the enthusiasm and confidence in the retarded that we in my work field share, decisions such as [mine] would be fewer. . . . Actually, if I were the only one involved, I would have kept the baby and used the best of my training to raise him. But to me the burden placed on the rest of the family, and on society, as I age or die, and the burden which in turn would fall upon the child, is too great to justify satisfying my ego.[37]

Moreover, women who undergo amniocentesis testing are put in contradictory relationships to the fetuses they carry. On the one hand, they are encouraged to bond with the "baby," to feel the baby move in their womb and take pleasure in its presence. On the other hand, however, these women must be prepared to consider aborting this "fetus" if an abnormality is detected. With amniocentesis, parental acceptance is often conditional on test results: "A diagnostic technology that pronounces judgments halfway through the pregnancy makes extraordinary demands on women to separate themselves from the fetus within. . . . This technology demands that we begin with separation and distancing. Only after an acceptable judgment has been declared, only after the fetus is deemed worthy of keeping, is attachment to begin."[38]

Such a relational pattern, I suggest, is produced in part by the relationships we have in contemporary American liberal society. We are encouraged to develop close bonds, but always provided those bonds do not extend across "unacceptable" boundaries such as the boundary liberalism draws to separate rational from nonrational beings or the public sphere from the private. This is true, I think, even in what we believe to be our most private and protected activities. Relationships established before birth in America thus only reflect the lifelong relational experiences engendered within our society. The way we relate to our fetuses becomes the way we relate to each other.

This emphasis on reason, I suggest, serves as the foundation not only for relational patterns between Americans, but for a philosophy which underpins the American legal subject as well. Reason divides human lives into the mutually exclusive realms of public and private —public being the world which all reasoning beings view as self-evident and can agree on, and private being the particularistic tendencies which are matters of personal taste. Although the reasoned subject of the public sphere is ostensibly universal and genderless, as I will explain in chapter 5, this public space in reality most closely resembles the world of white, propertied men. The desires and circumstances of many women—such as pregnancy—are not treated as public events, but rather as private, personal preferences. Moreover, the rational nature of this type of human subject demands that each person be understood as a unitary and organic whole. If what makes us human is our ability to reason, we cannot risk the disintegration of that criterion by accepting ideas that suggest we are fragmented or not entirely whole. As I will discuss in chapter 7, this fiction of the reason-based unitary subject undergirds the entirety of the contemporary abortion conflict.

CHAPTER TWO

The Catholic Construction of Abortion
Double Effect, Proportionalism, and Casuistry

◄○►

*As a Catholic, I speak for a large community that has a long
tradition of welcoming strangers and giving them a home, and of
holding itself up to judgment for the quality of that welcome; a
community which has learned painfully that the extent to which
we close our homes and hearts and lives to others, and especially
to children, is precisely the extent to which we have placed
ourselves beyond the reach of a loving God.*

Michael Garvey

In 1979, a Catholic woman from rural Pennsylvania, whom I'll
call Betty, became pregnant. She loved the baby's father and
would have married him, but he was already married to someone
else. Not knowing precisely what she should do with the rest of her
life, she moved to the nearest city, had her baby in a Catholic home
for unwed mothers, and left the baby with a nice couple from the
parish each day to search for work. She waitressed for a while and
had a few other odd jobs, but she grew increasingly dissatisfied with
her life, as well as with the life she was barely providing for her son.
One day, soon after the baby's first birthday, Betty simply didn't pick
the boy up.

Betty went home to finish college and then went on to graduate
school. She is now a friend of mine, quite a successful feminist

academic, and like me, no longer a Catholic. Of all the personal stories I heard in the process of writing this book—all the broken relationships, botched abortions, all the regrets—hers is the most painful.[1] She knew, she says, that her life ought to go somewhere, ought to be worth something. She also knew, she says, that she wasn't a very good mother. The couple from the parish provided a family to her child that she could not. After hearing Betty's story, I began to think about the young women I knew growing up who had made similar choices. Two girls dropped out of my class in parochial high school to have babies and at least half a dozen left the College of St. Rose to do the same. Most of these girls went to some other city to have their babies and then put them up for adoption through Catholic agencies.

While these decisions were undoubtedly painful, the women and girls who made such choices often did so because, as Betty articulated it, it was "part of her way to God." Inside the world of traditional Catholicism, a socially and theologically intertwined system of support exists which makes these decisions not only possible, but necessary. This system sustains these women and directs them against the "easier" solution of abortion, which they recognize as a sin. That is, because of the way traditional Catholics understand both the world and God, abortion is a fundamentally different moral event than that physically identical procedure in other contexts.

The Roman Catholic magisterium uses the philosophical principle of "double effect" to determine the only conditions under which abortion may be found acceptable. "Double effect" is a carefully reasoned, precise argument that enables one to judge, in situations where one action will have both good and bad effects, whether committing the action constitutes a sin. According to church teaching, abortions that are unintended, such as miscarriages, are not sinful. In order to guarantee that the evil consequence of a particular action is unintended, traditional Catholic moralists suggest that we must be able to describe the act without using the term "abortion" or any substitution for that term. That is, an abortion is only unintended if it can be defined as something other than an abortion.

There is little agreement about the origins of double effect theory. Joseph Mangan traces the principle to Aquinas, though he concedes that "it is not entirely clear that St. Thomas himself enunciates this principle."[2] He argues, though, that Aquinas implies the principle in his treatise on self-defense, *Summa* 2.2, q.64 a.7c. Other theologians, however, deny that the principle exists in Aquinas's works. As Josef Ghoos writes, "It is perhaps possible to find in Aquinas' work premises which permit one to deduce the principles of the act of double effect; but Aquinas himself does not seem to have formally elaborated or proposed the doctrine."[3] Ghoos, instead, argues that the doctrine of double effect appeared much later (beginning about 1575), formally outlined first in the work of John of St. Thomas in 1630. Regardless of when the principle was first articulated, it has gained widespread adherence over the centuries.

Currently, the magisterium finds only two types of abortive procedures morally acceptable under the dictates of double effect: the case of a pregnant woman with a cancerous uterus (the fetus is then removed along with the uterus) and the case of ectopic pregnancy, in which the fetus is lodged in a fallopian tube (the fallopian tube is then removed).[4] The indisputably unintended nature of these two exceptions is verified by the four conditions of double effect. The Catholic Church believes that by observing the parameters of these four guidelines, no Catholic will ever sanction an intended abortion.

1. *The act under consideration, independent of its context (action qua action), must be good or indifferent.* It is unacceptable, under this rule, to commit

or perform an evil to achieve an ultimate good. According to adherents of double effect, if the description of the act signifies an evil, nothing can make that act morally good or indifferent. One cannot, for example, kill John in order to prevent him from killing Mary, because killing, in and of itself, is an evil. If, however, John unjustly attacks Mary, it might be argued that the act under investigation is defensive; that is, the action that kills John can be defined instead as defending Mary. Thus, in this view, the evil described as "killing" drops out and the good action of "defending" takes its place. This semantic distinction ensures that any evils performed are wholly unintended.

2. *The moral agent must directly intend only the good effect of the action; the evil effect is only indirectly intended.* The intended effect (the one that is directly intended) must be morally good; only the unintended act (the one that is simply permitted) may be evil. As in the above example, the good of "defending" Mary must be the only one intended; killing John must be understood as simply permitted. This condition contains the logic that the entire principle of double effect is formulated to achieve; the other three conditions are designed to guarantee its smooth operation.

3. *The good effect is not produced by the bad effect.* In this condition, one must be able to narrate the actions under consideration such that the good effect happens before or simultaneously with the bad. If the good effect flows from the bad in a subsequent manner, the action could be understood as the commission of evil to achieve good. Thus, if there were any other way of defending Mary, or any contravening measures that would ensure her safety, the killing of John could not be understood, according to this criterion, as indirect.

4. *There must be a proportionately grave reason for permitting the evil.* Here, the effect of the good act must be evaluated against the effect of the bad and found comparatively greater. For example, it would be morally wrong to kill John because he was about to cheat on a test, for the moral evil of killing would be proportionately greater than the moral good of saving John from cheating. (Proportionalism argues that this consideration is the only valid one for moral decision making.)

In the licit cases of ectopic pregnancy and cancerous uterus, then, the criteria of double effect are met because (1) the removal of a pregnant cancerous uterus or pathological fallopian tubes is a good, or at least morally neutral, act; (2) the intention is to remove the disease, and hence the abortion is not an end in itself; (3) the removal of the defective organs can be called something other than an abortion; and (4) the abortion is proportionately permitted because it saves the life of the mother, which would otherwise be lost along with the fetal life.

Any abortion performed outside these two instances is considered illicit. Consider, for example, a pregnant woman who suffers from chronic hypertensive heart disease associated with severe renal insufficiency. If this woman does not receive an abortion, she will probably die from cardial or renal dysfunction brought on directly by the pregnancy. However, under the conditions of double effect, even though this woman may die, an abortion is unacceptable. Although she could argue that she intended merely to save her own life, under the logic of double effect, an abortion would violate criterion 3, because the good effect of saving her life would be produced by the bad—the abortion—which could not be called something else.

Although adherents rely on the principle because they feel it is philosophically sound, it is not coincidental that the restrictive conditions that double effect sets out for abortion perfectly express traditional Catholic understandings of the way that God works in the world. The philosophy that underpins traditional Catholicism in relation to abortion is enmeshed in a cultural system that the philosophical convictions both produce and are produced by. For example, traditional Catholics surround themselves not only with children, but with pictures of and prayers for centuries of saints; they create a "household of faith," which historian Ann Taves has described as a "network of affective, familial relationships between believers and supernatural 'relatives,'" a gathering that implies that life is designed to be lived in community, and that all should be welcomed.[5] In this context, abortion is wrong because no child is or ever could be "one too many." It is not that large families are the desired end of abortion prohibitions; it is simply that the existence and bounty of large Catholic families deny the very necessity of abortion.

As I argued in chapter 1, human bodies do not exist "out there," waiting to be organized into governing cultural systems. Rather, the logic of any system comes into being only within actual bodies, reproducing itself as it produces children. How many children we have, like their physical and mental characteristics, is determined by the size and shape of the space allotted within the ideological system that defines us. While the number of children in many traditional Catholic families may be in some respects a result of official interdicts against abortion and contraception, the size of these families also works to signify membership in Catholicism, and to reflect Catholic beliefs about God's work in the world. Just as the rational bodies produced by technological advances signify membership in liberal ideology, the bodies of seven or nine or perhaps even twelve siblings usually tell us something about where their family goes to church, and consequently what it believes. The issue of abortion in Catholic America must be understood in relation to this cultural identity. The space of big families, and the philosophies and interdicts that accompany them, are part of what it means to be Catholic. Identity is inscribed not only in individual bodies, but also in how many bodies configure a family. According to the way that Catholic theology sees the world, there is always enough to go around, always room enough for one more. Or as Dorothy Day, cofounder of the Catholic Worker movement, once suggested, "a baby is always born with a loaf of bread under its arm."[6]

The story of abortion and Catholicism in America, however, does not end with these large families. Over the past three decades, Catholic feminists have persuasively challenged the magisterium's teaching on abortion, birth control, and sexuality, arguing that the role of women in the church's social teachings is limited, restrictive, and misogynist. These challenges, especially with regard to abortion, have spawned large-scale altercations between the Vatican and many American Catholics. For example, on 7 October 1984, an advertisement in the_New York Times, sponsored by "Catholics for a Free Choice" called for open dialogue among American Catholics on the issue of abortion:

> Statements of recent Popes and of the Catholic hierarchy have condemned the direct termination of pre-natal life as morally wrong in all instances. There is a mistaken belief in American society that this is the only legitimate Catholic position. In fact, a diversity of opinions regarding abortion exists among committed Catholics.

This declaration incited unprecedented anger in many Roman Catholic Church officials because, in their opinion, it was erroneous. In their minds, official condemnation of abortion had always been utterly clear and absolute. In fact, the Vatican disagreed so strongly with the advertisement that it commanded all of the twenty-four religious signers to publicly retract their statement or face dismissal from their congregation. What this ad called "a diversity of opinions," American Catholic theologians called proportionalism. Furthermore, not only did the Vatican force the religious signers to recant, in its "Resolution on Abortion" the National Conference of Catholic Bishops in the United States claimed that "no Catholic can responsibly take a 'pro-choice' stand when the 'choice' in question involves the taking of innocent human life."[7] When American Catholics refused to follow this teaching, they increasingly found themselves denied communion, threatened with excommunication, or dismissed from their orders.

Until the Second Vatican Council (1962–65), moral theologians around the world understood that they were not to debate the validity of a ruling that the Vatican had pronounced, even when that pronouncement was not made ex cathedra. They might debate interpretations, but they could not challenge the teaching directly by favoring an alternative methodology. All this changed with Vatican II. Although the documents passed by the session took virtually no notice of abortion, the "new" spirit mandated by the council set the stage for much of the dissent that followed. The postconciliar Catholic, "while committed to the faith, [was] more 'independent-minded,'" as Richard Neuhaus puts it, "and quite prepared to challenge both governmental policies and church doctrine on matters such as birth control and premarital sex."[8]

Thus, by the time of the 1968 pronouncement *Humanae Vitae*—the encyclical that upheld the church's restrictive attitudes toward sexual matters—attitudes toward formal dissent had changed dramatically.[9] After Vatican II, many American Catholics felt it was not only their responsibility to dissent but also their Christian obligation to do so. As Maureen Fiedler, one of the "Vatican 24" (a signer of the *New York Times* advertisement), put it, "Adult, responsible Catholics have the right, even the duty, to speak out for what they believe is the good of the Church."[10] The *New York Times* ad, one of the first public declarations of dissent, grew out of this obligation.

Many American Catholic theologians responded by questioning and reformulating the philosophical foundations on which Catholic abortion interdicts were built. Thus, although double effect remains the only official method for determining licit abortions, many respected and thoughtful American Catholic scholars have spoken and written in favor of a different, unauthorized methodology.[11] Proportionalism, proposed in the current debates as a less rigid alternative to double effect theory, allows for abortions in many more cases. The term "proportionalism" is derived from the idea that evils must be weighed against each other and evaluated. Although still understood as sin, an abortion may also be understood as the lesser of two evils, and therefore sometimes morally acceptable. Just as the principle of double effect is endorsed and supported by the cultural precepts of traditional Catholic theology, the philosophical presuppositions of proportionalism are produced by and reproduce the convictions of assimilated American Catholicism.[12]

In 1968, Father Charles Curran asked the following question of double effect: If, according to Catholic thinking, an ectopic pregnancy can licitly be removed along with the pathological fallopian tube that holds it, why can't the fetus simply be removed from the tube, without taking the tube? As he writes, "By removing just the fetus, the doctor does not impair the childbearing ability of the mother. The doctor knows that the fetus has no chance to live and sooner or later will have to be removed. The logical solution would be to remove the fetus and save the tube if possible."[13] Double effect thinking permits abortion in the case of ectopic pregnancy only if the tube is also removed, for it is the pathological nature of that tube and its subsequent removal which allow the abortive procedure to be understood as unintended. What *is* intended is the removal of the pathological tube. Curran, in asking his question, bypassed the discussion of intent and moved directly to an application of proportional reasoning. In his thinking, a result that left a woman with her fallopian tube (and consequently her ability to bear children) intact was obviously preferred over one that did not. Curran's thinking reflects the idea that evil must sometimes be done to achieve good, an idea that is anathema to proponents of double effect.

A formal critique of the idea of intent associated with double effect was introduced by the premier scholar of proportionalism, Richard McCormick, in his 1973 Marquette Lecture, "Ambiguity and Moral

Choice." Here, McCormick articulated "dissatisfaction with the narrowly behavioral or physical understanding of human activity that underlies the [traditional] interpretation of direct and indirect."[14] McCormick's alternative construct forcefully interrogated the philosophical naiveté associated with intent, while it simultaneously reflected American ideologies. It is worth letting McCormick register his differences with double effect in his own voice:

> The rule of double effect is a vehicle for dealing with . . . conflict situations where only two courses are available: to act or not to act, to speak or remain silent, to resist or not to resist. The concomitant act of either course of action was harm of some sort. Now in situations of this kind, the rule of Christian reason is to choose the lesser of two evils. This general statement is, it would seem, beyond debate; for the only alternative is that in conflict situations we should choose the greater evil, which is patently absurd. This means that all con-crete rules and distinctions are subsidiary to this and hence valid to the extent that they actually convey to us what is factually the lesser evil. . . . Thus the basic category for conflict situations is the lesser evil, or proportionate reason.[15]

McCormick took Curran's practical application and developed it into a moral methodology that, as he claims, was self-evident, even for Christians. By rejecting intent as a measure of morality and relying only upon the consequences of an act to determine the act's acceptability, McCormick launched the discussion of proportionalism.

With these inquiries, Curran and McCormick proposed such major revisions to the strictures and application of double effect that a new methodology for ethical decision making began to emerge. For these thinkers, if an evil act produced good results that proportionately outweighed the evil results, the act should be considered licit; they advocated the use of only criterion 4 of double effect—"There must be a proportionately grave reason for permitting the evil"—

and rejected the first three criteria as futile attempts to establish intentionality. Proportionalists measure an act in terms of good and bad effect; if the good is comparably greater, the evil produced in the act is acceptable. Thus, the Catholic dictate to "do good and avoid intentional evil" is abandoned in favor of a methodology that places the moral weight on the comparative outcome.

The methodology of proportionalism is clearly opposed to the beliefs of traditional Catholics who hold that doing good and avoiding evil are duties that cannot be compromised or bargained away. The antipathy of traditionalists is expressed against proportionalism in a series of accusations that include relativism,[16] incommensurability,[17] and utilitarianism.[18] These denunciations and the proportionalists' responses occupy a major portion of the work in contemporary Roman Catholic moral theology. At stake in this conflict is not only method but authority, not only philosophical principles but cultural identity. The disagreement between traditionalists and proportionalists reflects the conflict waged over who it is that American Catholics owe allegiance to, Roman Catholic ideology or American. As William Spohn writes, "Often today the charge of being a 'proportionalist' means only that the theologian does not agree with the magisterium that certain . . . acts should be prohibited absolutely."[19]

The most significant methodological difference between double effect and proportionalism can be viewed in cases where a therapeutic abortion is the only means of saving a woman's life (also known as life-against-life dilemmas). In the logic of double effect, abortion is to be avoided at all costs, often even if the costs include the mother's life. Here, a mother's faithfulness to God's commandments carries more moral weight than her life. Even if a mother dies in childbirth, as long as she did not seek an abortion she can rest assured that she did not sin. In the logic of double effect, it is better to allow one woman to die—or if you are the pregnant woman, to die yourself—

than to kill a fetus.[20] Or as many moral theologians and church officials have articulated, two deaths are better than one murder.

Proportionalists are unwilling to accept such exacting criteria. They promote awareness of and adaptability to multifaceted dilemmas and are willing to allow certain evils for the attainment of higher goods. In most life-against-life situations, proportionalists believe that one death, even if it is accomplished by the sin of abortion, is better than two. Although abortion performed under these conditions is clearly evil, proportionalists can consider certain abortions as not necessarily sinful if they are formulated to be less evil than the other choice. Although significant developments in medicine— most specifically Cesarean section—have rendered most of these life-against-life situations obsolete, the methodological difference between these two ways of configuring moral behavior remains remarkable, particularly because proportionalism's primary audience resides in America and is largely defined by its values.

American Catholics, according to recent statistics, are practicing birth control and abortion at rates rivaling those of Protestant and secular America. Gallup polls indicate that a large percentage of American Catholics support legal abortion.[21] Kristin Luker claims that "as a group, Catholics are increasingly using contraception in patterns very similar to those of their non-Catholic peers."[22] As more and more American Catholics find abortion necessary, the intellectual space for a relaxed theory such as proportionalism widens. It is not that proportionalists write in direct response to the increase in Catholic abortions; rather, these events and beliefs emerge together in a growing pattern of what it means to be an American Catholic.

The ideology of a specifically American Catholicism has coincided with changes in the American Catholic family.[23] Catholics, if they want to become more American, have fewer children. My paternal grandmother, for example, who immigrated here from Eastern

Europe when she was sixteen, raised her six children and cared for her elderly mother-in-law in a small two-bedroom house in Syracuse, "up near St. Vincent's Parish." After she died, my father gave the house to my soon-to-be-married brother and sister-in-law for their first home. Frank and Sue lived there happily until their first child came along, but wanting more room, they soon moved to the suburbs, selling the house to Sue's single brother. His visitors now often remark on how perfect the house is for someone who lives alone. The changes that this little house has undergone reflect the transformation of my Catholic extended family into a more typical American one. The desire to enjoy the benefits of liberalism prompts many Catholic families to use abortion and contraception to control the size of their families.[24]

In his influential history *The American Catholic Experience,* Jay Dolan argues that Catholics have stood, not in opposition to American ideology, but rather in a free and happy relationship, participating fully in American life.[25] If public values conflict with religious beliefs, Catholics are usually able, according to Dolan, to lay aside their "private" religious convictions. Assimilation into American life is made possible by the separation of church and state. As part of "church," Catholic morality is perceived as a personal characteristic or conviction acceptable only if it does not conflict with the larger precepts of the state. Allegiance and obedience to an ethic that pervades all aspects of life—such as the principle of double effect—appear in Dolan's narrative as "an old-world, European model of Catholicism."[26] In the "new and exciting, thoroughly American Church," Catholics respond to tensions and anti-Catholic sentiment by publicly proclaiming their loyalty to everything the Republic stands for: individual choice, freedom, pluralism, and democratization. This new American church blends beautifully into the existing American landscape.

Dolan's narrative indicates the influence that American liberalism has had on contemporary American Catholicism. Indeed, at the close of his history, Dolan suggests that pluralistic attitudes have given new life to Catholicism in America: "There is no longer one way to do theology, to worship at Mass, to confess sin, or to pray. There are various ways of being Catholic, and people are choosing the style that best suits them."[27] Catholics today are able to choose "the style that best suits them," I suggest, only because their particular choices do not conflict with the overarching loyalty that Catholics must, in this narrative, grant to America. The portrayal of these theological "options" as one thing among many to be consumed in accordance with personal taste poses no threat to the primary allegiance America requires, that is, the conviction that the ability to make free choices is more important than the content of any particular choice.[28] Choosing the style that best suits them mirrors the liberalism upon which proportionalism is founded.

This "new" Catholicism, then, differs from the traditional not only in that it offers the space for personal choice, but also because such personal choice (as long as it is in keeping with the values of the liberal state) can be considered moral even if it conflicts with traditional Catholic values. Because allegiance to the Republic is formulated as the most fundamental moral value, pluralistic Catholics are allowed to choose the values of America over traditional Catholic values with a clear conscience. This wedding of American liberalism and Catholicism dictates that particular religious commitments are acceptable only in private, and only as long as they do not conflict with the overriding commitments made, in the public arena, to the presuppositions of American ideology. Proportionalism emerges today in the American Catholic Church as a result of attempts to reconcile traditional tenets with American liberalism.

The benefits of proportionalist methodology for American Catholic women, who no longer need assume unlimited duties of childbearing and childcare, are patent. Proportionalism, along with the shift toward Catholic assimilation into mainstream American culture, offers women the freedom to pursue careers and other interests unhampered by unwanted familial commitments. Catholic women have managed to liberate themselves through abortions sanctioned by proportionalism, which is itself sanctioned by American liberalism. However, while the opening up of choices outside the home clearly represents an advance for many women, other options for women have been closed off.

For example, fewer Catholic families envision their lives as being intertwined with those of the unwed pregnant mothers in their parishes largely because there are fewer women with full-term unwanted pregnancies. Because more women rely on abortion, the systems that previously existed to support women with "unwanted pregnancies" have been virtually disassembled. Before abortion was legalized in America, most Catholic parishes sponsored or supported homes where women could go to have their children. Catholic adoption agencies and Catholic social services existed in most geographic areas as back-ups for those women who couldn't find housing for themselves or a welcoming family for their children. When an unmarried, pregnant woman went to her priest for the sacrament of confession or simply for guidance, the priest was immediately able to incorporate her into these systems. However, these networks of Catholic caretaking have been either greatly diminished or completely dismantled. Where once the priest knew precisely where to send a woman with an unwanted pregnancy, now he is increasingly less certain about what her options, and her moral obligations as a Catholic, are.

This situation is not unrelated to the liberalism which underpins the choices modern women have made. The logic that mandates that religious particularities be cordoned off into the private sphere also dictates that we must sequester particularities associated with female-ness or womanhood. Liberal ideology makes it acceptable for us to be women, perhaps even feminists, as long as we do so in private spaces and only as long as these commitments don't interfere with our prior (more important) commitment to keep such particularities out of public, political space. The traditional Catholic systems which supported women with unwanted pregnancies have disappeared because women in liberal ideology are perceived as self-sufficient, iso-lated individuals. Private needs and affiliations, such as pregnancy and religion, are cordoned off into the private sphere.

What has been lost in the shift to proportionalism is the ability to respond to an unwanted pregnancy in the way that Betty did. In some ways, Betty had more options than "being pregnant" or "not being pregnant"; she had a way to deal with her situation that allowed her to be responsible both to her baby and to the family she called her church. Betty had the option of turning her baby over to a circle of care that was more often than not centered in her parish. Betty gave her son up not precisely because she couldn't care for him, but because she knew firsthand that someone else would care for him better. With all of its faults and oppressive tendencies, she found the community which enabled this decision within the fabric of tradi-tional Catholicism.

My own biological mother did as well. She carried me—un-wanted—and turned me over to Frank and Rosamond Rudy, Catholics like herself, to raise. She did this because, as a traditional Catholic, she saw the world as a place where there would always be room for one more child, where "family" is more about sharing faith than sharing a household, and where sharing a household expresses such faith. My biological mother believed in a God who is accommodating and loving enough to provide for everybody, and she lived in a family founded not upon blood relations but rather on these theological convictions. In taking me in, my adopted parents taught me the virtue of welcoming a stranger and showed me how to see my church, both my local parish and Catholicism worldwide, as one family. Even though my political quarrels with the Catholic Church have been severe enough to cause me to leave it, I also mourn the loss of the community and ideology which sustained Betty and my mother.

In their influential *The Abuse of Casuistry*, Albert Jonsen and Stephen Toulmin propose an ethical methodology to break the headlocked debates between traditionalists and proportionalists, a methodology which may reap the best of both worlds. They argue that "[m]uch of the current abortion debate has been carried on in terms that appeal to certain supposedly universal principles, from which the participants deduce practical imperatives that they regard as applying invariably and without exception."[29] Such is certainly the case with proponents of both double effect and proportionalism. Each side has a rule—"never do evil to achieve good" versus "always act to avoid the greatest evil"—which each claims exemplifies Catholic moral principles and intuitions. Jonsen and Toulmin suggest that such abstractions are not ultimately useful in many cases of morality. Casuistry, the moral methodology they endorse, relies not on abstract rules or principles, but on the moral intuitions which emerge in the resolution of particular cases.

As Jonsen and Toulmin define it, casuistry is "the analysis of moral issues, using procedures of reasoning based on paradigms and analogies, leading to the formulation of expert opinions about the existence and stringency of particular moral obligations, framed in terms of rules or maxims that are general but not universal or invariable, since they hold good with certainty only in the typical conditions of the agent and circumstances of the action."[30] Jonsen and Toulmin suggest that when people set aside their principles and maxims, they are usually able to come to some agreement about concrete decisions, even if they disagree regarding the principles that support those decisions. Rather than relying on a specific rule or principle to resolve a situation, casuists would have us evaluate its contours and circumstances against other cases already successfully resolved. As they argue,

> The heart of moral experience does not lie in a mastery of general rules and theoretical principles, however sound and well reasoned those principles may appear. It is located, rather, in the wisdom that comes from seeing how the ideas behind those rules work out in the course of people's lives: in particular, seeing more exactly what is involved in insisting on (or waiving) this or that rule in one or another set of circumstances. Only experience of this kind will give individual agents the practical priorities that they need in weighing moral considerations of different kinds and resolving conflicts between those different considerations.[31]

Rather than holding ourselves to the binding maxims, Jonsen and Toulmin suggest that we surrender our attachment to rules and instead employ "the art of practical resolution of particular moral perplexities."[32] Thus, casuists might deliberate on the morality of any particular abortion not by extracting solutions from principles, but rather by inquiring about the concrete conditions of the case. It is not that maxims should be disregarded, but that they should simply be understood to have limited value in determining the outcome of certain cases.

Although, as I will demonstrate momentarily, the casuistrical method is limited in its ability to deal with abortion cross-culturally, it is a method worth investigating precisely because it begins to pay attention to contexts in the investigation of morality. Differing greatly from the methods introduced by both the principle of double effect and the theory of proportionalism, contemporary casuistry relies on the context of an act for its moral evaluation. As Jonsen and Toulmin write, "Circumstances . . . are the integers to be added up in the description of an action: add or subtract one relevant circumstance, and the act may have to be described, named, and evaluated in quite a different way from before."[33]

Casuistry had its origins in the Roman Catholic practice of penance, which, as Jonsen and Toulmin note, began in the fifth century as superiors of monastic communities began assigning particular penalties to community members after they had publicly confessed their sins. By the sixth century, private confession to a priest had become the norm for many lay Christians. In an effort to help the clergy assign appropriate penances for these confessions, casebooks called "penitentials" were written. These books, Jonsen and Toulmin argue, constitute the earliest examples of casuistry. The penitentials did not include maxims or moral platitudes, but suggested instead practical taxonomic categories regarding the "circumstances of the case." After hearing a penitent's confession, the priest referred to the cases listed in the penitential and ordered the appropriate penance. While the earliest penitentials were bare lists which "rarely went beyond the citing of a scriptural or patristic text to justify the penitential verdict, "by the twelfth century, casuistry had become a full-blown scholarly endeavor entailing attention not only to the sin committed but to the way the sin was described, the conditions of the commission, and the character and position of the agent.[34] The later manuals reflected the complexities that arose when differing circumstances surrounded what had previously appeared to be the same sin.

Casuistry appears to offer a resolution to the contemporary

Catholic abortion debate because it attends to the context of an act without jettisoning the ability to make concrete claims about morality. That is, the casuistrical approach does not suggest, as does proportionalism, that it is acceptable to do evil in order to achieve good. Rather, casuists propose that, when circumstances are taken into consideration, a sin can often be redescribed in order to give a penalty (if necessary) that is more in keeping with the spirit of the act than with the letter of the law. Thus, for casuists, it is not the case that evil can be considered good as a result of its relation to a given end, but rather that a seemingly evil act may be understood, in a more nuanced light, to be a different (and even, at times, acceptable) act. This allows casuists to maintain the categorical distinction between good and evil while making what they deem to be necessary "commonsense" exceptions. As Anscombe describes it, "[Casuistry] deal[s] with a borderline case by considering whether doing such-and-such in such-and-such circumstances is, say, murder, or is an act of injustice; and according as you decide it is or it isn't, you judge a thing to do or not. . . . [W]hile casuistry may lead you to stretch a point on the circumference, it will not permit you to destroy the center."[35] Thus, Anscombe supports casuistry because it retains the ability to make moral judgments while allowing for certain exceptions. Additionally, the methodology enables priests to address the needs of women who—like Betty and my mother—want to respond to their perception of a generous God and turn to the Catholic communities that sustain their belief (and that will no doubt sustain their children). Casuistry, then, can be understood as a third alternative in the American Catholic debate about abortion. On the one hand, casuistry satisfies the desire of traditional Catholics to hold certain moral maxims steadfast and secure; on the other hand, casuistry also offers the kind of flexibility that is advocated by proportionalists.

However, in the contested world of Catholicism at the turn of the twenty-first century, casuistry has difficulty accounting for the differences between the way that these competing ideologies understand and construct the act of abortion. In providing a method that can appeal to both factions, Jonsen and Toulmin tacitly assume that both sides share a common history of intuitions and convictions regarding moral behavior, a common way of understanding precisely what abortion is.[36] In regard to abortion, they assume that only one, unified act exists, and that everyone involved can agree upon its parameters. As American Catholics move closer to the ideology of American liberalism and further away from traditional understandings, this commonality is harder to achieve.[37] Increasingly, American Catholics and Roman Catholics function as contending moral communities which see the world—and its moral problems—quite differently. Because casuistry can only be successful when common understandings and meanings exist, it has limited usefulness in the contemporary abortion debate. As long as there are insurmountable differences between proportionalists and traditionalists, between American and Roman Catholicism, casuistry will not work. As long as Catholics disagree about the shape of the world, they will not agree on which rules ought to be retained or when they ought to be bent. Casuistry will not work unless it is grounded within the parameters of a concrete tradition. It is not enough simply to pay attention to context; that context must be seen as existing within some framework of intelligibility, within some ideology.

The way Catholics see the world, and what they see in it, changes from community to community. In chapter 6, I will outline how casuistry might help to bridge the current divide between traditional and modern believers. Today, however, the differences between these two ideologies seems philosophically and culturally insurmountable. While it was once fairly clear what a practicing Catholic with an unwanted pregnancy should do, the range of possible solutions for assimilated Catholics has radically changed. American Catholics have contracted a new set of practical reasonings regarding morality, a new collection of convictions regarding the place of abortion in the modern world, a new history supporting their identity. This new identity is formed not only within the growing proportionalist challenge, but in the struggle between Rome and the American church as well. As a recent headline in the *National Catholic Reporter* proclaimed, "Gallup Poll Indicates that U.S. Catholics Disagree with Vatican over Practically Everything."[38] Even casuistry cannot easily account for or negotiate such a chasm.

CHAPTER THREE

The Function of Abortion
in the Rescue Movement

—<o>—

*During a rescue mission, a group of believers obeys God's
command to rescue the innocent, saying "No! We're not going
to let you kill innocent children." The rescuers peacefully but
physically place themselves between the killer and his intended
victim. This is done in a number of ways. They may enter the
abortion procedure rooms before the patients arrive and lock
themselves in. They may fill up the waiting room or they may
come before the abortuary opens and block the door with their
bodies, their cars or special locks, so that no one can get in. It
can be quite exciting and a little frightening. In any event,
rescue missions win a stay of execution for the baby.*

Randall Terry

Before Randall Terry involved himself in the issue of abortion,
almost all rescuers, leaders, and strategists of the opposition to
abortion were Roman Catholic. Two Catholic groups in particular
made rescue attempts prior to the founding of Operation Rescue.
Joan Andrews's Pro-Life Abolitionists League attracted approximately
forty members to at least two local rescues and represented a nonviolent approach to direct action. Indeed, as part of their ministries,
Andrews and her friends took pregnant women in need of help into
their homes and provided free food and shelter for dozens of women.
Joseph Scheidler's Pro-life Action League attracted even fewer mem-

bers, but it advocated more aggressive actions against abortion clinics. Scheidler's book *Closed: Ninety-Nine Ways to Stop Abortion* has been linked to bombings and other illegal actions common before the founding of the national organization. Both of these Catholic groups were small, and according to one reporter, "easy to dismiss... as a strictly Catholic [phenomenon]."[1] The founding of Operation Rescue, however, made dismissal of rescues much more difficult.

In 1984, Randall Terry, a used-car salesman, founded "Project Life." Thirty members of this nascent organization picketed their first abortion clinic later that year. More significant than the rescue itself, however, was the fact that Terry had tapped into a new population of anti-abortion activists: evangelicals.[2] Terry connected his own conversion and personal commitment to Jesus Christ to his growing concerns about abortion and preached an evangelically oriented anti-abortion message wherever and however he could. By claiming that God requires evangelical Christians to stop abortion, he renewed the political convictions of this segment of Christianity and paved the way for evangelicalism to dominate anti-abortion activities. Terry helped other evangelicals focus on and identify with "the baby" as an extension of their unwavering commitment to Christianity. As a result of his appeal, rescuers now agree that God has directly called them to stop the destruction of babies. Rescuer Paul deParrie explains, "Rescues are necessary because of the command from God."[3] Indeed, all members of Operation Rescue attribute their involvement in the movement to theological origins.

Under Terry's influence and preaching, Operation Rescue remains an evangelical movement. Terry himself estimates that more than 60 percent of Operation Rescue is evangelical, while the remaining 40 percent is split between Catholics and mainline Protestants.[4] By 1986, Scheidler and his Pro-Life Action League had been integrated into Operation Rescue (although Scheidler remained behind the scenes owing to legal difficulties). Terry had, however, rejected Scheidler's tactic of illegal invasion in favor of a less aggressive blockade, a move that allowed individuals with commitments to nonviolence—such as Andrews—to endorse Operation Rescue. Even though Scheidler and Andrews deeply disagreed about anti-abortion strategies, Terry's nascent organization was able to incorporate both groups because of its radical Christian orientation.

Terry founded the national office of Operation Rescue in Binghamton, New York, in 1987. As Terry's wife explained, "When people were praying about it, that's when Randy felt that the Lord gave him the vision, or whatever you want to call it, of being in front of abortion mills across the country and just shutting them down, hundreds of thousands of people just shutting them down all over the country."[5] Operation Rescue's first effort attracted more than three hundred participants to Cherry Hill, New Jersey, in November of 1987. Soon after Cherry Hill, members of Operation Rescue began to distinguish themselves from what they called "passive pro-lifers," from the more mainstream pro-life movement. The identity "rescuer" was forged by the movement's more zealous wing.[6]

Despite the fact that Operation Rescue received little support from the mainstream pro-life movement, the rescuers succeeded in popularizing the practice of civil disobedience in the crusade against abortion. Prior to the organization of the national movement, fewer than 1,000 people had been arrested for interventions intended to prevent abortion. After the national office opened, however, more than 55,000 were arrested. But because these arrests resulted in more than $70,000 in court and legal fees, a cost that the national organization was unable to bear, the national office closed in 1990. Rescue missions are now conducted only by local organizations. While Randall Terry remains committed to the work of rescuing, he no longer operates a central headquarters for the movement. As one reporter put it in November of 1991, "What the public and press regard as a single organization under Terry's thumb is now a loose-knit confederacy of local anti-abortion groups that Terry, still a respected strategist, influences but does not control."[7] This decentralization allows the rescue movement to continue without incurring large debts.

Operation Rescue's success is due in no small part to its affiliation with the New Christian Right. Although the contemporary Christian right is currently interested in a wide variety of moral and "family values" issues, the issue that first drew the New Right together was, in fact, abortion. As far back as January 1979, Jerry Falwell and other anti-abortion Christians were meeting to discuss the idea that America would never fully realize its Christian potential unless the sin of abortion ceased. By forming the Moral Majority later that year, Falwell hoped to persuade those Christian Americans who believed that abortion, homosexuality, premarital sex, gambling, and women's liberation were immoral to organize themselves. In so doing, Falwell was the first major evangelical figure to translate Christian action into conservative political involvement; to be an evangelical Christian in America, according to Falwell's Moral Majority, meant joining forces with party politics to eradicate immoralities. In the years that followed, this affiliation was to shape the character of both the Republican party and evangelical Christianity.

Evangelicals had actually already begun to get involved with party politics in the 1976 election of "born-again Christian" Jimmy Carter. At a time when most of the country was skeptical about Carter's religious affiliations, evangelicals came out in full support of this Democratic candidate. However, as Marsden writes, "[d]espite his evangelical credentials, Carter's liberal Democratic politics soon proved unpopular with many . . . evangelicals."[8] By the 1980 campaign, evangelicals, assisted and organized by the Moral Majority, were ready to stand behind a different candidate, one who shared their growing concern for the Christianity of America: Ronald Reagan. In the 1980 presidential debates, Reagan appealed specifically to evangelical sentiments as he claimed, "I have always believed that this land was placed here between two great oceans by some divine plan. It was placed here to be found by a special kind of people. . . . I have found a great hunger in America for a spiritual revival, for a belief that law must be based on higher law, for a return to tradition and values that we once had."[9]

With such rhetoric, Reagan won the hearts of many American evangelicals and cemented the relationship between conservative Christians and the Republican party. This relationship is important not only because the visibility of the New Christian Right inspired many evangelicals to participate actively in actions like Operation Rescue, but also because, in many ways, it made the popularity and visibility of the rescue movement within the wider American public possible. Without the rise of the New Christian Right, Operation Rescue might have been understood and dismissed by the media as simple religious fanaticism. The Republican party persuaded many evangelicals that Christianity's rightful place is in politics, and Operation Rescue provided a forum for such religiously motivated public action outside the sphere of electoral politics.

Republican leaders in the early Reagan years encouraged preacher-politicians such as Falwell to enter the political arena. These Christian figures could deliver votes, funding, and the resources of twenty-seven organizations, such as the Moral Majority, the Christian Coalition, and the 700 Club, to Republican candidates. In return for this support, leaders from the Republican party met regularly with these ministers and, in many cases, took seriously their concerns regarding the immoral attitudes that had taken over America. In some cases, as with evangelist Pat Robertson, conservative Republicans even encouraged Christian leaders to run for office themselves and supported them with advice and election plans. Although it challenged the moderates in the Republican National Convention, the primary purpose of Robertson's campaign for the 1988 Republican presidential nomination was to shore up evangelical support for conservative party politics. Equally important, the Robertson campaign, as Randall Terry claims, secured evangelical participation in future elections: "In the late '80s and early '90s, we're seeing a whole new wave of Christians come in[to politics]. . . . Rev. Pat Robertson's presidential campaign brought out of the pew and into the process tens of thousands of new people, many of whom are still involved. Their full impact will not be felt until the 1996 election, the 2000 election, 2004."[10] The central message of the Robertson campaign was simply that Christians should be involved in American politics. Built on the efforts of political Christians throughout the decade, Robertson's campaign organized a significant number of Christians into party politics and established a network of grassroots connections and organizations. It was these contacts that were deployed when the national office of Operation Rescue shut down; the grassroots organizing that had been done enabled the rescue movement to continue at the local level.

Robertson's campaign and Falwell's ministry created this widespread, grassroots network not with organized religion's traditional tools (books, magazines, direct mail, church-related groups), but largely through television. Fundamentalist and other Christians in all parts of the country became accustomed to watching for Robertson's messages regularly on their TV screens. Americans watching these evangelists were told that the morality of America was deteriorating, and that Christians should be doing something about it. At the same time, these same viewers then turned their channel to the evening news and saw Christian "rescuers" actively participating in the campaign to free America from the immorality of abortion. This message that Christians should be involved in politics was extended to the realm of morality by Operation Rescue.

The televised link between conservative Christianity and Republican party politics cleared a path for many Americans to both understand and accept, if not support, the rescue movement. This triangular relationship was sealed when Jerry Falwell entered the rescue movement at its frenzied height in Wichita in the summer of 1991, bringing with him not only a donation of $10,000 for bail money, but multitudes of reporters and cameras as well. Falwell intended to demonstrate just how far Christians would go in their fight for morality, and this is precisely what America saw: conservative Christians, like Terry and Falwell, rescuing. Although conservative Christians often decry contemporary technology and suggest that the American media is biased against them, Operation Rescue itself has received an unprecedented amount of media coverage.

This aggressive use of television by both Operation Rescue and the New Christian Right has, according to many scholars, radically simplified the complexity of the Christian message. "Cast in the form of an easily communicated narrative," writes Quentin Schultze,

> the story of the Creation, the Fall, Redemption, and the Second Coming could be summarized for even the most uneducated and illiterate audiences. This narrative structure provided inherent (television) audience interest, especially compared with religious messages relying heavily on doctrines or systematic theology. . . . [Televised religion] is intended to make it [as] easy for audiences to accept the faith as if it were the latest consumer product.[11]

Nowhere is this simplification process more apparent than in the Christian Right's representation of abortion. The average Christian viewer of an Operation Rescue news story is told, "God knows that abortion is wrong."[12] On television, abortion is a "yes or no question," something viewers are either for or against.[13] Arguments that take complexity, life experience, and extenuating circumstances into account—like those discussed in chapter 2—are completely absent. Once an individual is convinced that abortion is wrong, involvement in anti-abortion activities such as Operation Rescue seems to be the only just option. "If abortion is murder, why aren't we treating it as such?" is the popular refrain of Randall Terry and other conservative rescuers. This kind of appeal has succeeded among many Christian viewers who often see the act of sending a check or making a phone call as helping to revive America's dormant faith. As Robert Wuthnow comments, TV watchers "can return petitions about abortion and see Falwell carry them to the White House."[14]

The right or wrong formulation of the abortion issue parallels the spiritual simplicity presented in televised Christianity. When a televangelist asks if viewers are "right with God," he expects an answer unencumbered by uncertainty or ambivalence. Like abortion, salvation is a "yes or no issue"; the only way to "get right with God" is to support the issues and campaigns authorized by that preacher and the New Right. Scholars have found that such simplicity is particularly appealing when patriotic identification seems unstable. In a country that seems shaken by pluralism and diversity, televised Christianity offers some Christians a haven of moral certainty. As William McLoughlin writes, "The spokesmen for the Christian Right are offering millions of Americans something they want very much to believe in—an assurance of renewed commitment to traditional values, myths, and doctrines and thereby a return of God's protection and guidance."[15] Thus, the logic of televised Christianity appeals to Americans who feel that the nation has lost its moral center. By participating in organizations like Operation Rescue, evangelical Christians can save the country and, in the process, themselves.

In his analysis of evangelical culture, Grant Wacker suggests that the evangelical right is "functionally defined by its commitment to the rebirth of Christian civilization in America."[16] This conservative evangelicalism hopes to transform America into a Christian nation, into a country which would, as Randall Terry states it, "self-consciously try to build [its] laws and institutions around the principles and laws of the word of God."[17] Pat Robertson links this hope to the abortion issue when he claims that "[i]f we continue to buy the arguments of radical feminists . . . the unrestrained abortion of America one day will lead to the wrath of God descending on this land that we love so much."[18] Similarly, rescuers display pictures of aborted fetuses swaddled in the American flag to represent the downfall of the nation. Encased in the patriotism of the flag, these dismembered fetuses are intended to represent national crimes of immorality. Our only hope of salvation, according to these dark images, comes from our attention to those prophets who will help our nation recover its Christian heritage.

The rhetoric that combines Christianity with patriotism extends back to the era of the Puritans and has been present in different formulations since the founding of this country. The present commitment to a "Christian America," however, is unique in that it takes the form of political participation and indeed entails a commitment to particular candidates. Moreover, the tactics in the electoral arena reflect the oversimplifications of televised Christianity. Like the New Christian Right's attitudes toward salvation and abortion, voting, too, is constructed as a straightforward choice between right and wrong. As Randall Terry succinctly stated it, "A vote for Bill Clinton is a sin."

Many conservative Christians have become extremely skeptical about the idea that society is moving forward. What others see as advances toward higher or better ends—evolution, sophisticated criticism of the Bible, pluralism—are seen by conservative Christians as leading society down the path of faithlessness and away from the Kingdom of God. Society, they believe, is on a road that leads straight to hell. While individuals may be redeemed in history, history itself is doomed; only God's forceful and extreme intervention will save us from eternal damnation. In this "premillennialist" theology (in which it is believed that God's judgment will be rendered before the millennium described in the Book of Revelation), most fundamentalists accept that humanity—which includes the earthly church—is getting worse, not better. Human progress cannot inaugurate the reign of harmony; rather, the coming of the heavenly kingdom is entirely up to God, who, upon Christ's premillennial return, will separate those who have been faithful to his gospel from those who placed their faith in worldly things. The fundamentalists believe that righteous Christians must continually do battle with the evil forces of history in order to be chosen as one of the elect at Christ's return. This battle, as they see it, is waged between the evils of science or enlightenment and the truth of the Bible; Christians must follow the inerrant teachings of Scripture above all else in order to be saved when God sorts out the faithful from the damned at the end of time. This premillennialist orientation is explicit among the conservative factions of Operation Rescue, among those members who believe that the world is so immoral that only direct intervention on God's part will bring about the peace and happiness.

Thus, premillennialist Christians have become involved with Operation Rescue, I suggest, not to bring about the eschaton directly, but rather to distinguish themselves as "saved" in the eyes of God and the nation when the eschaton comes. It is possible to read the rhetoric regarding Christian America as being concerned not with the salvation of the nation as a whole but with "the faithful" alone. By supporting candidates that "Jesus would have chosen," members of the Christian Right establish themselves as moral and spiritual leaders of the country, and therefore as the faithful remnant who will be saved when the end-times come. Contemporary fundamentalists do not seek to avoid the world to save their souls; rather, today's logic encourages these Christians to be active in the world and in politics in order to substantiate their own salvation.

The issue of abortion, then, functions as a kind of litmus test for salvation among many rescuers. For them, the people who will be among the saved at the end of time will be those Christians who put their faith into particular kinds of action; salvation is virtually guaranteed to those who have risked embarrassment and arrest in the rescue movement. What is at stake for these conservatives is not just an individual fetus, but eternal salvation itself. Premillennialist Christians involve themselves in the issue of abortion not only to save the unborn but also to save themselves.

However, other ideologies do exist within the movement. Although the leadership of the national network is largely conservative and premillennialist, competing belief structures can be found if the surface is scratched. Many participants in Operation Rescue are affiliated with what Grant Wacker calls the "evangelical left," which advocates a more open and inclusive Christianity where "freedom of inquiry, the open market of ideas, cultural and artistic liberty and human technologies" are encouraged. The evangelical left includes, he claims, "most black and perhaps a fourth of white evangelicals," among them "theologians like John Howard Yoder and Clark Pinnock; scholars like David O. Moberg and Timothy L. Smith; activists like Jim Wallis and Jon Alexander; public figures like Mark Hatfield and John Anderson; organizations like the Berkeley Christian Coalition and Koininia Farm; and magazines like the Wittenberg Door and Daughters of Sarah."[19] Perhaps what defines these

Operation Rescue members is the fact that their desire to rescue is rooted not in premillennialism or American exceptionalism, but rather in an extension of the nineteenth-century reform impulse. In the postmillennialist theology associated with the nineteenth-century abolition and temperance movements, God orders Christians to bring into the "new creation" such outcast groups as slaves, prisoners, the intemperate, and now, the unborn. By working toward justice and liberation, human beings themselves can help to bring about the Kingdom of God. For these Christians, abortion activism is just one of the many ways that they can heed God's call.

For example, rescue worker Juli Loesch started out her political career by working for the United Farm Workers grape boycott in California and Detroit in 1969. She then moved into the communal living and full-time peace work at the Pax Christi Center, a leftist Christian organization which operates as a nonviolent meditation and action group. Loesch has been living there for the past nine years and says that "[a]nyone who [can] tolerate our prayer life is welcome to move in."[20] Although her primary concern is, as she calls it, "no nukes," she also considers herself a feminist. Loesch has been arrested four times for her attempts to rescue "babies" from abortion. As she claims, her involvement in both peace and rescue activities allows her to "work both sides of the aisle. We preach no-nukes to the pro-life movement," she says, "and anti-abortion to the peace movement." Loesch refers to herself as a "fetus-loving peacenik," a label which even pro-choice advocate Connie Paige claims "does convey something of her uncompromising spirit."[21] For Loesch and others, rescues are undertaken as an extension of their involvement in postmillennialist theology. These people translate evangelical-ism into support for liberation movements and service projects; in other parts of their lives, the left rescuers are involved in soup kitch-ens, "meals-on-wheels," community organizing among the homeless and powerless, and direct and indirect social action against war and nuclear arms. In their view, working against abortion is another way of working toward liberation and the heavenly kingdom.

Thus, in the frame of the postmillennialist rescuers, abortion is not an issue used to define and mark participants as "saved," but rather a problem whose solution will help bring about the harmonious living God intends for us all. Although abortion is wrong, it is just one of many social ills needing healing, not the sin upon which the millennium will be decided. Women who seek abortions and even doctors who perform them aren't direct enemies but are themselves caught up in processes of corruption and sin.

The opposition that exists in Operation Rescue between progressive reform impulses and conservative ideologies is not without precedent in the evangelical house, but it is particularly poignant within the issue of abortion. While all rescuers are politically opposed to abortion and are willing to take public action against the procedure, the reasons that stand behind that seemingly unified opposition vary greatly. Operation Rescue is a community in conflict. Although its members come together for rescue events, they in fact share very few theological foundations.

For my part, I believe it is our duty as Christians to help bring about the justice and liberation exemplified throughout the Scriptures and Christian history. God calls us to work toward a better world; salvation will occur within history, not in being redeemed from it. In terms of both theology and practice, I believe that our churches could and should be working to alleviate the injustices that make abortion necessary. As I will argue in chapter 6, I don't think many of our congregations address this goal very well. We are much too quick to take on and identify with the secular categories of pro-life and pro-choice, an impulse which obscures our ability to work together to end this oppression. Thus, although for reasons

I'll explain later I do not endorse rescuing as a Christian intervention, I do believe—along with the leftist rescuers—that alleviation
of the many sufferings associated with abortion ought to be the practice and intention of every Christian community.

CHAPTER FOUR

Conflicted over Men, Women, and Sex

Abortion in the Frame of Contemporary Feminisms

◄o►

> *From the outside, "feminism" may appear monolithic,*
> *unified, or singularly definable. The more intimately one*
> *becomes acquainted with feminist criticism, however,*
> *the more one sees the multiplicity of approaches and*
> *assumptions inside the movement.*

Robyn Warhol and Diane Price Herndl, *Feminisms*

Not everyone concerned with women's oppression and liberation agrees about the role of abortion in women's lives. Although most self-identified feminists favor the availability of safe abortions, they do so in a number of different ways, with different needs, interests, and political concerns in mind.[1] These differences affect not only the way these women view "abortion," but also influence what factors they take into account when they evaluate its morality. While few feminists believe that abortion is ethically wrong, they believe radically different things about the institutions and practices that surround abortion, as well as about how the problems of sexism might be solved. Underneath the seemingly unified feminist consensus, a variety of conflicts exist regarding the nature of men, the nature of women, the value of children, the role of the family, the role of government, and the pain and pleasure of sexual intercourse.

Indeed, in the last decade, many of us have come to realize that no one thing called feminism accurately exists, that we no longer have "feminism," but rather "feminisms." As we shall see, these differences have profound implications for the discourse of abortion.

The history of the movement that eventually legalized abortion is inextricably intertwined with the history and development of the contemporary women's liberation movement. However, this "women's movement," like the feminisms that followed, was not seamless, but fraught with conflict over many aspects of the abortion issue. In various juxtapositions, feminist groups often stood in stark conflict with each other on many issues. Not surprisingly, the conflicts that accompany feminist struggles today very often mirror the issues that arose during the development of women's liberation, in particular, issues revolving around sexuality. When we examine the history of abortion in the past three decades through the lenses of contemporary feminisms, it is clear once again that the meaning of "abortion" depends on a complex web of social circumstances for its meaning and valuation.

Although abortion had been deemed a criminal act during the Physician's Crusade of the 1870s, the medical profession continued to terminate pregnancies legally in situations in which abortions were "medically indicated."[2] Because such diagnoses were often complicated and uncertain, and because they were usually left to the discretion of individual physicians and administrators, a great deal of variation existed in abortion practice. In some cases, abortions were only performed to save the life of the pregnant woman; in other cases, the definition of "therapeutic" was broadened to include abortions for women who claimed that their pregnancy caused emotional distress or who threatened suicide if they didn't receive the abortion. Very often, therapeutic abortions were performed for those who had either the capital or social connections to influence the doctors and administrators who made such decisions, while women who lacked such resources had to rely on illegal abortions. Inconsistent medical judgments produced erratic methods and standards for therapeutic abortion. By the late 1950s, these discrepancies had come to the attention of people both inside and outside the medical profession. As a result, legislators attempted to regularize abortion by moving abortion decisions out of the domain of medicine and into the domain of American law, adding yet another meaning to the complex set of interventions we call "abortion."

In 1959, in an attempt to regulate medical abortions, the American Law Institute drafted a set of guidelines designed to help determine the conditions under which a woman should receive an abortion. This bill was prompted and supported by doctors and hospital administrators. Under it, a pregnant woman would present her case to a hospital abortion committee, and she would be granted an abortion if the pregnancy was determined to be a result of rape or incest, if the pregnancy endangered her physical and mental health, or if the fetus was defective.[3] Although the bill seemed to offer solutions to some of the problems associated with abortion, several incidents intervened before it could be standardly adopted.[4] These events persuaded the American public that the responsibility for abortion decisions should be moved out of the realm of medicine entirely.

In 1962, Sherri Finkbine, a middle-class mother of four and host of the *Romper Room* television series, became pregnant for the fifth time while taking the tranquilizer thalidomide. Although thalidomide was not marketed in America, it was widely available in Europe and was often prescribed for the nausea and nervous tension sometimes associated with pregnancy. It was quickly discovered, however, that thalidomide caused severe abnormalities in many fetuses, including retardation and defective physical development (very often producing flipper-like appendages). Finkbine's physician advised and scheduled an abortion. The night before she was to receive her medically authorized procedure, Finkbine phoned the local newspaper, the *Arizona Republic,* and requested that they print a warning to other pregnant women regarding the disastrous side-effects of thalidomide. She told her story to the paper in hopes that it would alert other women in a similar situation. When she got to the hospital the next day, however, she found that the publicity had alarmed officials, who refused to allow the abortion even though her physician was fairly certain that her fetus was deformed. (In Arizona in 1962, therapeutic abortion was legal only to save the life of the mother, and although exceptions were often made to this rule, the Finkbine case had already received so much attention that the hospital felt it could not publicly challenge the law). Finkbine's physician requested a court order to perform the abortion (claiming that the abortion would indeed save the mother's life), and although the judge granted it, no hospital would perform the procedure until the laws were clarified. The Finkbines were forced to go to Sweden for their abortion, after which it was determined that the Finkbine fetus had indeed been severely deformed.

A similar scenario occurred two years later with an outbreak of German measles. In 1964, more than twenty thousand deformed babies were born as a result of rubella-infected pregnancies. As with the Finkbine case, physicians and hospitals often responded more to the fear of legal prosecution than to the needs of pregnant women. And in many cases their fears were not unfounded; in some states, doctors who performed rubella abortions faced loss of license and even further prosecution.

Meanwhile, it was becoming increasingly clear that while abortion was largely unavailable to women with defective fetuses, it was increasingly available to women with extensive socioeconomic resources. These "legal" abortions that were performed for upper-middle-class white women were managed in a number of different ways. Sometimes, private doctors slipped such procedures through the loophole of "life-saving abortion" by (mis)diagnosing the pregnancy as a threat to the woman's life. In other cases, the woman was instructed to claim that if she did not receive an abortion she would commit suicide; she would then receive her abortion for psychiatric indications. Other times, a woman who had a long-standing personal relationship with a physician might receive her abortion without ever naming it as such. Her physician might schedule her for a routine D and C (dilation and curettage), a procedure used to clean the uterus of tumors and abnormal growths, but which would also produce an abortion.[5] All of these abortions were dangerous for the physician, and were thus reserved for patients who could pay large fees.

The Finkbine and rubella incidents, coupled with the fact that certain women often received safe and ostensibly legal abortions, underscored the inequities involved in medical abortions. Only women with money and social connections could get abortions; poorer women with legitimate needs—such as those with defective fetuses—were regularly denied. Awareness of these discrepancies helped to galvanize health, social service, and law professionals into what became the first branch of the contemporary abortion movement.

This awareness coincided and resonated with several other cultural shifts of the 1960s. Swept up by the tide of anti-war and civil rights demonstrations, women began to demand power over their own lives. During this period, an increasing number of women left bad marriages, married later, delayed childbearing until their careers had been established, and attended college. Simultaneously, and related to these changes, women began to think about their own sexuality differently. The development and marketing of the birth control pill had for the first time given them an unobtrusive way of controlling their fertility, ushering in the "sexual revolution." Women's sexual lives seemed freer because men could no longer complain that they "didn't want to break the mood" or that birth control "felt unnatural." Furthermore, the pill could if necessary be taken without men's knowledge. The problem of course, was that the pill didn't always work. Moreover, it was often difficult to obtain, especially for poor women.[6] The result of inadequate birth control and inadequate access to safe abortion was that often only women were punished for participating in this new sexual climate. Every woman of childbearing age who had sex with a man (even with birth control) ran the risk of unwanted pregnancy. If she became pregnant and could not obtain a medical abortion, she would either have to change her life to accommodate an unwanted pregnancy and perhaps an unwanted baby, or often more tragically she would be forced to seek an illegal abortion.

As women came to understand their own sexualities and capabilities and fought for their right to choose when and under what conditions they would bear children, they increasingly sought illegal abortions to end unwanted pregnancies.[7] And frequently, these abortions proved fatal. Thus, a growing number of people became concerned not only with the injustices associated with the health care system, but with the increasing number of deaths of women as a result of unsafe, illegal abortions. They were outraged at the fact that they and their friends had to risk their lives to receive abortions, when the same procedures performed in hospitals were completely safe and virtually trouble-free. By the mid 1960s, abortion rights groups had organized and constituted a large faction of contemporary American feminism.

From 1967 to 1973, the contemporary women's movement flourished through the work of women who had learned organizing tactics in leftist political groups, self-proclaimed "radical feminists."[8]

These women were patently dissatisfied with proposals set forth by the medical industry to regulate therapeutic abortion, as these proposals left abortion in the hands of institutional medicine. Only women themselves could decide whether or not to use their bodies to bear children, they asserted. No board or doctor should prevent them from obtaining abortions. For these women, abortion was solely a female issue; the only subject involved in the issue was the pregnant woman herself.

Although these early feminists belonged to, learned their tactics from, and were indebted to New Left organizations, their relationship to the left was troubled. For the most part during the sixties, the left was organized by men who were slow to be persuaded that women, too, could take on roles of leadership. As Robin Morgan writes, "Thinking we were involved in the struggle to build a new society, it was a slowly dawning and depressing realization that we were doing the same work *in* the Movement as out of it; typing the speeches men delivered, making coffee but not policy, being accessories to the men whose politics would supposedly replace the old order."[9] Thus, although one of the hallmarks of the New Left was the idea that there is a political dimension to personal life, the movement was largely unable to grant that political dimension to the personal lives of women. As a result, many women broke rank with the left to organize the first branch of the contemporary feminist movement, and they did so by focusing on the issue of abortion.[10]

These new feminists would be satisfied, not with the legalization of abortion, but only with the repeal of all laws outlawing abortion. Ninia Baehr explains the difference between legalization and repeal:

> If you repeal something from the law, you take it out of the law entirely. If you legalize something, you grant control to the state. For example, alcohol is legal in this country, but the government doesn't trust each person to regulate her own relationship with alcohol. It tells

her how old she must be to drink it, when and where she may buy it—and it changes the laws about alcohol as it sees fit. This is not true, say, of orange juice. The criminal code does not mention orange juice. The government lets us drink it when, where and how we want to. The FDA still checks to make sure that the orange juice is safe. The government will even help us pay for our orange juice if we receive food stamps. Other than playing this supportive role, the government is silent on the matter of orange juice. Repeal activists wanted the orange juice situation, not the liquor situation, when it came to abortion. They knew that as long as the government maintained a voice in each women's abortion decision, it would use that power to chip away at women's right to abortion. Clearly, their predictions have come true with a vengeance.[11]

Just as they steadfastly refused to be dominated and overshadowed by the men of the New Left, these women refused to be controlled by the men of medicine. As Ellen Willis states it, these feminists sought

> not merely formal equality for women but genuine self-determination. Our target was not only those who opposed abortion altogether but the growing ranks of (mostly male) reformers, who proposed to allow the (overwhelmingly male) medical profession the right to grant abortions to "deserving" women in limited circumstances—rape, substantial threat to health, likelihood of fetal deformity, and so on. The issue, we insisted, was not how cruelly or compassionately a male dominated society should treat women with unwanted pregnancies, but women's moral right to control their fertility and therefore the direction of their lives.[12]

This cry for self-determination and repeal demanded safe and open access to abortion for all women. It hoped to ensure that women would be able to pursue careers and educations, and to participate freely in the sexual revolution without running the risk of pregnancy. Women should be able to obtain abortions at all stages of pregnancy, they argued, regardless of the condition of their pregnancy, their ability to pay, or their standing in society.

Many of these feminists didn't wait for the slow wheels of government to turn on proposed legislation. As Ninia Baehr writes, "Abortion activists have a rich history of taking the law—and their lives—into their own hands. When the law doesn't respect women, women don't respect the law."[13] Feminist organizations, local women's health networks, and even groups of concerned clergy found a number of ways to get around legal restrictions. First, because so many illegal abortions had resulted in women's deaths, these services attempted to locate and refer women to sympathetic doctors who would perform legal medical abortions on women inside hospitals for reduced rates.[14] Although all hospitals had guidelines regarding medical abortions, many doctors had become adept at manipulating these parameters for wealthier patients; the early feminists were simply asking the doctors to extend their service to poorer women. Second, when such connections faltered, these groups began to refer women to physicians who performed abortion in locations where the procedure was either legal or unregulated, primarily Puerto Rico, Mexico, and England. Problems arose here because referral services could not usually monitor the conditions of foreign clinics; women often arrived home no better off than if they'd had the back-alley abortions which had spawned the need for the referral service in the first place. Third, grassroots organizations referred women to illegal domestic abortionists who were thought to be safe because they had appropriate medical training. In some cases, doctors who performed abortions inside hospitals had supplemented or moved their practice outside the hospital in order to avoid suspicions or to escape regulatory problems; others had freely set up independent practices in order to increase their incomes. Still others had problems getting licensed in a particular state, or in finding jobs; illegal abortion was a way for them to continue to practice medicine. Because these doctors often lived and worked in the same geographic areas as the referral systems, their operations could be monitored for safety, reliability, and cost.

Feminists sometimes discovered that a "doctor" who was routinely performing abortions in fact had no medical training at all. When this happened, the referral service might try to direct women in need to other locations, eventually forcing the untrained abortionist out of business. But this wasn't always the case. Abortion activists realized that the safest abortions were often performed not by doctors, who were frequently rushed and expensive, but by women and midwives who offered a supportive and healthy emotional environment as well. These practitioners were far different from the inexperienced and uncaring abortionists who had caused the deaths of countless women. JANE is perhaps the most famous example of this type of service.[15] Located in Chicago, this group of feminist women began by referring women to someone they thought was a doctor. This "doctor" asked the women of JANE to assist him in the abortions he performed; the women of JANE, through observing the simple procedures this doctor employed, thus received inadvertent training. Eventually, when JANE learned that this high-priced abortionist wasn't a doctor at all, they realized that they could perform abortions themselves. As one member of JANE explained, "I can do things that I never felt I could do. All that crap about how you have to be an expert, it's just a ruse to make you feel incompetent in your own life."[16] During the four years that these women performed inexpensive, safe, nonprofessional abortions, no woman was turned away for lack of money. Moreover, JANE had a safety record equaling that of licensed providers in the state of New York after abortion was legalized.

By the early 1970s, several feminist referral services and support groups had begun to explore the possibilities of nonprofessional abortion. Abortion, it was argued, was not a medical procedure at all, but was a natural part of women's history, and when left to women, the procedure could be executed safely, cheaply, and easily. Indeed, an extension of this ideology can be found even today in the growing popularity of "menstrual extraction," a procedure which women perform on each other monthly to artificially extract menstrual blood (and any fetal tissue).[17]

From the perspective of these pro-abortion feminists who wanted full control over abortion, the victory won with the *Roe* decision was a compromise; although it legalized abortion in the first two trimesters, women still did not have the absolute right to control their bodies. Access to abortion was still dependent on male approval because doctors, hospital administrators, and judges, who were usually male, still controlled the circumstances, such as length of pregnancy and ability to pay, under which safe abortions would be performed. From the pro-abortion perspective, the "pro-choice" rhetoric was itself a compromise. As Rosalyn Baxandall argues, "the phrase 'the right to choose' was actually a step backwards, a compromise with the growing right wing who used the better-sounding slogan 'the right to life.'" Baxandall continues,

> In the women's liberation movement of the 1970's we asked for total repeal of all anti-abortion laws and free abortion on demand. During this period [the late sixties and early seventies], we referred to forced pregnancy as slavery. Feminist lawyers argued that criminal abortion laws imposed a formal servitude that violated the 13th amendment, which ended slavery. This was a stronger, less ambivalent argument than the right to privacy. It was clear that abortion was a woman's rights issue and a necessary condition for women's autonomy. In the late 1980's and early 1990's, abortion began to be referred to as a human rights issue and the life referred to was abstract. Without this emphasis on female rights, we leave the door open for a discussion of fetal rights and parental consent. It's almost as if in the 90's people are

afraid either to use the word abortion, or to state that abortion is a female issue. Abortion and feminism have become dirty, shameful words. So we use the word choice and speak of parental and human rights. This is a sign we have become defensive and are losing ground to the neo-conservatives.[18]

Pro-abortion feminism was bound up with the political and sexual struggles of the 1960s. These early feminists largely favored the sexual revolution and participated in abortion politics precisely because they thought sex was good and they wanted to have more of it more safely, that is, without the fear of pregnancy.[19] Full access to abortion would liberate women sexually and, some thought, would disrupt the stronghold of male supremacy. By the mid 1970s, however, a significant number of feminists began to assert that having sex with more men more often only forced more women to go to clinics more frequently. Thus, the pro-abortion feminism of the late 1960s and early 1970s began to give way to a second school of thought.[20] Although many women remained convinced of the need for repeal of abortion laws, their numbers diminished over time. By 1975, all of the signal pro-abortion feminist groups had officially disbanded— although the Redstockings reassembled and continue to operate a small organization. Their burnout was due in large part to the tensions that arose between them and the New Left, and between them and the next wave of feminists. While groups in the earlier movement supported the idea of women's equality to men in the workplace and in matters of sexuality, many of the newer feminists focused more on women's differences, arguing that, when released from oppressive sexual relationships with men, women's special capabilities of nurturance and caring could be exercised more freely.

Feminists in both camps wanted the same thing: control over their own reproductive capacities. But they went about achieving this goal in two entirely different manners. The earlier feminists believed that the institutions of medicine and law could not be trusted to proceed with women's best interests in mind. These institutions were not responsible enough to set up systems of birth control and abortion which would meet the expanding needs of liberated women. The second group, in an attempt to secure control over their own bodies, disassociated liberation from heterosexual intercourse. For them, freedom meant the ability *not* to have sex with men, and therefore not to get pregnant. The first branch of feminists targeted institutions such as capitalism, consumerism, medicine, and government as enemies that perpetuated the sex-class system and accepted husbands, brothers, and male friends sympathetic to the women's movement as sexual partners and as partners in the struggle. The second branch deemphasized institutional oppression and instead attributed sexism to the behavior and attitudes of each and every individual man. In this thinking, no man can be trusted; only other women can understand and participate in women's liberation.

Women involved in this second wave of feminism invested themselves less in changing male-dominated institutions such as the economy, medicine, and law, and focused instead on developing and celebrating women's culture. From their viewpoint, male culture was oppressive and violent; the only hope for a feminist future lay in a social reconstruction based on the values and moral structures of women. In this feminism, women are configured, not as equal to men, but as superior and as having an ethical duty to safeguard civilization from the course of doom and destruction ushered in by patriarchy. The words of poet Adrienne Rich capture this valorization of women's lives and bodies:

> I have come to believe that female biology—the diffuse, intense sensuality radiating out from clitoris, breasts, uterus, vagina; the lunar

cycles of menstruation; the gestation and fruition of life which can take place in the female body—has far more radical implications than we have yet come to appreciate. Patriarchal thought has limited female biology to its own narrow specifications. The feminist vision has [often] recoiled from female biology for these reasons; it will, I believe, come to view our physicality as a resource, rather than a destiny. In order to live a fully human life we require not only *control* of our bodies (though control is a prerequisite); we must touch the unity and resonance of our physicality, our bond with the natural order, the corporeal ground of our intelligence.[21]

Rich's writing, and the words and music of dozens of other feminists from this era, celebrated women's bodies, women's lives, women's experiences. These women attempted to reverse society's evaluation of genders by placing women on top, at the pinnacle of human existence.

The construction of women's nature as superior to that of men had ramifications for attitudes toward sexual intercourse with men. While the first feminists of the 1960s viewed sex positively and advocated abortion so that sex with men would not lead to forced, unwanted pregnancy, the feminists of the 1970s believed that sexual intercourse with men was at the root of women's oppression. Andrea Dworkin argued that women do not control the sexual act, that "every woman . . . lives inside this system of forced sex. This is true even if she has never personally experienced any sexual coercion."[22] The goal of these feminists was to liberate themselves from this sexual servitude by creating a female subculture free of men and free from the threat of male oppression. As a result, feminism of the 1970s was marked by increased acceptance and even a deliberate embracing of same-sex relationships. The earlier feminists had believed that lesbianism could never become fully feminist, as Ti-Grace Atkinson put it, "lesbianism involved role-playing . . . and reinforces the sex class system."[23] For the later feminists, however, sex with other women was the safest and most acceptable kind of sex; in a culture where men are considered the enemy, the choice of sexual partners became one of the utmost political concerns.

From many perspectives, this separatism appeared to be an advance. First, more feminists appeared in more places; events such as concerts and poetry readings, establishments such as women's bookstores, and various other configurations of "women-only" spaces seemed to provide a haven in which women could examine the state of their liberation while reflecting on and rehearsing the dangers of patriarchal culture. Second, in this separatist ideology, female gendered selves required neither compensation nor equalization; being a woman meant being strong and caring, and most important, not dependent on men.

Others in the movement felt, however, that such trends diluted the passionate politics spawned by the early activists. As Alice Echols explains, "although the [second branch] grew out of the [first], it contravened much that was fundamental to it."[24] From the perspective of pro-abortion feminism, these separatist women were involved in a countercultural movement aimed not at changing the dominant gender stereotypes, but simply inverting them:

> [U]nlike [the pro-abortion feminists] who typically rejected as sexist the whole idea of opposing male and female natures and values, [separatists] treated gender differences as though they reflected deep truths about the intractability of maleness and femaleness. By arguing that women are more nurturant, less belligerent, and less sexually driven than men, cultural feminists have simply revalued dominant cultural assumptions about women.[25]

In Echols's narrative, the second stage of feminism failed to carry through the political agenda set in motion by the first.[26]

For Echols, this failure is deeply intertwined with the fact that the later feminists focused largely on lifestyle, on separating themselves from men in all facets of their personal life: "How one lived one's life, not one's commitment to political struggle, became the salient factor."[27] From the perspective of the pro-abortion feminists, lesbian separatism was not a political act at all but an escape into a utopian fantasy. Echols notes with disdain that separatist women "'worked on their car all weekend,' as though it were an act of great political significance."[28] For Echols and her feminist sisters, politics meant marching, leafleting, protesting, and organizing against injustices in the public sphere, not fixing one's car. However, those whose primary goal was independence from men, taking over traditional "male" jobs (such as car repair) could be understood as the ultimate political act. Anything that allowed women to be free of men carried the revolution one step further.

Feminists associated with the separatist ideology thus placed a relatively small value on political interventions designed to grant women greater access to both heterosexual intercourse and abortion. They understood abortion as an extension of male dominance, a way for men to promote their own sexual pleasure, a method that men used to get women to have sex. Catherine MacKinnon, for example, suggested that abortion practices "let men and society off the hook," that "[r]eproduction is sexual, men control sexuality, and the state supports the interest of men as a group. [The legalization of abortion] does not contradict this."[29] Seeking a world in which men could no longer oppress and abuse women through sexual coercion, many of these feminists argued that men legalized abortion mainly for themselves. True liberation therefore meant becoming a "woman-identified-women." Issues that involved men, such as abortion and birth control, were avoided in favor of what was thought to be the more radical politics associated with coming out as a lesbian. In the political world of these feminists, abortion had largely become unnecessary. Although many of them did participate individually in the political struggles associated with abortion, many more left the what they thought of as the male-identified, public arena of abortion to effect political changes in their personal lives.

By the mid 1970s, most of the activists of pro-abortion feminism had either dropped out of the political scene or had been converted to the ideology of the separatists. The cry for repeal of abortion laws had all but died out as most of the women involved in feminism spent their political energies elsewhere. Indeed, for the first few years of legalized abortion in this country, there was relatively little feminist activity or discussion on the subject, which took a back seat to the concerns of alternative women's culture. This all changed when the national pro-life movement was born. Although the separatists continued to have a broad-ranging effect on feminism in general, the issue of abortion itself came to be dominated by a new breed of feminists.

Soon after and in direct response to the legalization of abortion, anti-abortion coalitions began to organize with a vengeance. Local and national "right-to-life" groups with a wide range of religious and political affiliations formed. These pro-life groups demonstrated the political power of single-issue campaigns as well as the intensity of the public opposition to abortion. A similarly strong response was needed to combat the pro-life movement, a response that would organize a wide variety of feminists into various levels of activism. The "pro-choice" movement was born.[30]

While some of the membership of the emerging "pro-choice" campaign came from the dying ranks of the pro-abortion movement, most of those involved in the abortion issue after 1973 had few direct ties to either the first or second waves of contemporary feminism. However, the women who came forward to take up the fight for access to safe abortion after *Roe* were often the beneficiaries of the social changes brought forth by the earlier activists. Specifically, many had careers, a right for which the pro-abortion feminists had fought. By the mid 1970s, the feminist movement had made it possible for many women to have meaningful work outside as well as inside the home; and although they couldn't devote themselves to full-time organizing, many of these women involved themselves in politics by making financial contributions to the issues that seemed most liberating to them.

The pro-choice movement thus found its funding base. Organizations such as the National Abortion Rights Action League targeted these women for fundraising by providing information in glossy packages and "memberships" that required only a contribution of money. Women could belong to feminist organizations without sacrificing either work or family time. Moreover, from the beginning, the pro-choice movement argued that abortion should be legal because family planning was a private concern; this argument appealed strongly to a generation of women who were the first to attempt to juggle families and careers. Thus, the social constraints faced by this group of feminists fashioned the pro-choice campaign into a broad-based, single-issue movement.[31]

The turn to single-issue politics was facilitated by the consciousness-raising associated with earlier forms of feminism. According to many commentators, feminism had largely succeeded in raising the consciousness of American women. As one woman put it, "We had the feeling that we were, like Columbus, sailing at the edge of the world. Everything was new and intense. But after a while we'd had all the breakthrough experiences."[32] Women were now well aware of their oppression, and they needed to translate that awareness into political action. Single-issue politics filled this function. Thus, groups of feminists in specific geographic areas became interested in issues such as women's health, equal pay, battered women, feminist race relations, rape crisis, and the Equal Rights Amendment, and they organized task forces and boards to oversee the correction of these problems in their local communities.[33] Abortion was only one of many social issues supported financially by these new career-minded feminists.

The media contributed to the portrayal of feminism as a movement that addressed a variety of isolated issues rather than as an organic, radical movement. Where once the media highlighted the more passionate (and often outrageous) aspects of women's liberation, by the late 1970s, they most often portrayed professional women such as Gloria Steinem and Betty Friedan as spokeswomen and leaders for the entire women's movement. Although many feminists from the second branch (and even some from the first) were still active in various cultural affairs, the message that America got from the news was that these liberal-minded career women represented modern feminism, and that anyone could become part of the movement with minimal effort. These images, along with the fact that it was relatively easy to "join" these organizations, caused an explosive growth in the feminist movement by the late 1970s.

This emphasis on the growth of feminism and on single issues such as abortion was supported by established organizations and interest groups, such as Planned Parenthood and the American Civil Liberties Union.[34] The political work of abortion took on a different orientation from that of the earlier pro-abortion activists largely because the women involved in the pro-choice movement had different expectations about how change would occur. Moreover, the pro-choice women had both the money and the skills to work within existing systems. Those women who joined the pro-choice movement identified with and trusted the paid professional feminists who lobbied in Washington because many of them worked in similar legal, corporate, or professional settings. As Suzanne Staggenborg notes, "abortion movement leaders were not 'outsiders' lacking access to political power holders. . . . rather [these pro-choice feminists] had the skills and connections necessary to work through established channels."[35] Thus, feminist political tactics surrounding the issue of abortion shifted from grassroots actions such as providing abortions or abortion referrals to more mainstream tactics such as congressional lobbying. Several feminist organizations who held socialist ideologies also participated in the abortion struggle; for reasons discussed at length in chapter 5, their impact was not as great nor their message as far-reaching as that of the liberal feminists who dominated the discourse.

What was lost in this shift to single-issue politics was the sense that one organization could conceptualize and strive for a feminist utopian ideal. In the 1960s, the majority of women who worked to help institute changes necessary for women's liberation did so on a full-time basis; in the 1970s, although the work was much more focused on personal development, women devoted much of their time to bringing about changes that they believed would support liberation. The single-issue politics of pro-choice required a much smaller commitment from feminists. Campaigns were designed so that the majority of women could support the issue without changing any part of their daily lives. For them, *Roe v. Wade* didn't represent a compromise but a victory for women; the task was to ensure that the pro-choice ideology of *Roe* remained intact. The rationale for the *Roe v. Wade* decision—privacy—buttressed the pro-choice model of the contemporary feminist as someone who was successful in public or professional life, but who also demanded the right to private, untouched, domestic space. The pro-choice movement attempted to bring about changes in women's lives by working completely within the American political and legal system. As

Staggenborg writes, pro-choice activism was "decidedly nonconfrontational" as local and national organizations targeted the legal system as the site of political change. These nonconfrontational tactics were "calculated to win support from mainstream Americans and established organizations."[36] No attempt was made to link abortion to a broader set of women's issues.

The single-issue model has gained even more widespread support in the aftermath of various anti-abortion proposals, movements, and organizations. In light of various threats from conservative legislators, it became more and more important to defend *Roe*. Even many feminists who had previously been involved in more radical movements responded by supporting abortion as a separate issue. As one feminist stated, "I have always been very much against single issue [organizing], but the horror of what was happening in 1980 with the New Right made me realize it was necessary."[37]

I suggest that abortion in the pro-choice frame is primarily understood as a procedure which enables women to participate equally in public life and therefore ought to be legal. With abortion, women can pursue careers with the same passion and determination as men; no woman should be denied professional advancement because of an unwanted pregnancy. In the rhetoric of the pro-choice movement, women have a right to abortion because women have the right to participate in the public sphere. Abortion in the frame of pro-choice is the issue which will ultimately help women lead more complete and fulfilling lives because they will have the ability to control their reproductive capacities. In focusing so intently on this one issue, however, I believe that the pro-choice movement has sacrificed some of the more organic transformations associated with earlier forms of feminism, in which women's liberation was seen as a series of reconfigurations in our understandings of the relationship of men, women, and sex. Although it has a broad base and wide membership, the pro-choice movement fails to address many broader concerns.

Clearly, different feminists have different views about the nature, function, and role of sexuality, and correlatively competing ideas about the morality, necessity, and meaning of abortion. I began this chapter by suggesting that most self-identified feminists were "pro-choice," and I conclude by suggesting that "pro-choice" doesn't mean only one thing. For some, the language and ideology of the pro-choice movement represents a compromise which limits women's ability to be fully sexually liberated; because the state still regulates abortion, women have a limited control over their own bodies. From another perspective, pro-choice is an abstraction that is a different kind of compromise, as any woman who is truly liberated would never need an abortion. Finally, for many, a pro-choice position toward abortion serves to signify membership in an amorphous community of feminism in America today; a whole generation of feminists mark themselves and identify each other with the ideology of pro-choice.

At an academic dinner party recently, I was part of a conversation about the importance of feminism in the university. Although most of the guests were tenured faculty members, not one had the reputation of teaching or conducting research in feminist lines of inquiry. I wondered precisely which kind of feminism they were endorsing for academia and precisely how it functioned in their lives and work. At the time, I was writing the Operation Rescue chapter of this book, and when I mentioned this, their responses helped me to see what was at stake for many of them in the constellation of feminisms outlined above.

Weeks before the dinner party, the NOW legal defense fund had sent out a massive fundraising letter which detailed the recent and flagrant crimes executed by the rescue movement. Everyone at the dinner party, save one, had received the letter. And almost everyone responded to it with a financial contribution. One woman admitted to having two abortions while she was in graduate school, and testified to the importance of supporting NOW so that abortion would remain safe, legal, and available. Another suggested that she had sent her money in because she was tired of only talking the feminist line; she wanted "to put her money where her mouth was." And a third remarked that she thought this would raise a lot of money as "all feminists were sure to support the cause." I asked them if they had ever considered attending a counterdemonstration against the local Operation Rescue. One informed me—patronizingly—that she hadn't gotten tenure by spending her Saturdays marching around; another told me that she didn't think such a confrontation was an appropriate place for her children; a third admitted, sheepishly, that she would be too scared. While feminism certainly does not hinge on counterdemonstration attendance, these comments reveal that for many women today, feminism entails only sympathetic allegiances coupled with financial support; no political organization is deemed necessary.

I tell this long and involved story of competing feminisms, as well as the more abbreviated story of the dinner party, as a way of introducing the next section. Turning my attention away from the project of contextualizing the meaning and morality of "abortion," I take a closer look at the ideology which currently dominates feminist thinking on the issue. By examining the liberal foundations of the movement, we will see some of the limitations of pro-choice ideology for feminists today. In the end, I suggest, the practices and beliefs associated with earlier formulations of feminism—particularly with the ideology of materialist feminisms—offer much deeper, richer, and more radical understandings than do the language and logics of the pro-choice movement. I also look at the limitations of the current debate for another community, the community of the Christian church. As I've outlined above, both feminism and Christianity have helped to form my views on abortion. In the next section I discuss how today's abortion debate limits the ethics associated with both communities.

PART TWO

THE LIMITATIONS OF THE CURRENT DEBATE

—◦—

CHAPTER FIVE

The Uneasy Marriage between Feminism and "Pro-Choice"

◄○►

*In trying to hold onto past gains, the pro-choice movement has
failed to pursue new ones, either by solidifying its own membership or speaking out to the public.* Roe v. Wade *was not the first
step of a feminist agenda for reproductive control; it turned out to
be the only step, defended by appeals to the right to privacy.*

Marlene Gerber Fried

I was eleven years old in the summer of 1967, but the growing
political unrest of the outside world seemed unreal to my sheltered Catholic life. The nuns who taught me through grade six all
seemed like versions of my mother and my aunts; they were kind to
children, helpful to each other, innocent, and above all, they all knew
their place. My mother turned her television off and quietly prepared
dinner when my father got home from work in the same way that
the nuns stepped to the back of the classroom when "Father" made
his weekly appearance. I secretly hoped that I'd turn out different
from these women, but up through the sixth grade I had no idea how
I could break such a mold.

But that fall, the events of the outside world came crashing into
my life in the form of my seventh-grade teacher, Sister Janice. Sister
Janice was also a nun, but she had nothing in common with the nuns

who preceded her in my life, let alone with the wives and mothers in my extended family. Sister Janice had just come back from Vietnam; she had been in jail for protesting the war; she had taken Vatican II to the extreme and dressed like (what my parents called) a hippie; she had been to Selma. When she taught, she didn't use books or notes, but would stand up in front of the classroom and challenge us to have the courage to dream dreams of justice. She took us to soup kitchens and jails as part of our social studies class. She had a light in her eyes that drew us in when she told us about Martin Luther King's mountain. She taught us to sing "Blowing in the Wind," "Teach Your Children," and "The Times They Are A-Changing." Sister Janice opened me to a world of justice-seeking passion; I was making connections and felt—perhaps for the first time—alive.

Sister Janice, and several others who came after her, led me down a long, sinewy march through the Catholic left, a path that eventually dumped me into the arms of feminism. For a young, sheltered, and scared woman coming of age in turbulent times, the Catholic left provided stability as well as radicalness, both of which I craved. Dan Berrigan, Caesar Chavez, and Dorothy Day were considered a new breed of saints who were honored for challenging institutionalized oppression while remaining firmly within the embrace of one of the most powerful institutions in the world. I was out of college two years before the commitment to social justice which they had instilled in me began to conflict with the church to which they belonged.

When I go to job interviews at Catholic colleges today, I tell them that I left the church over the issue of women's ordination. This is an answer that most reasoning American Catholics today accept; they nod their heads appreciatively and don't hold my Methodism against me. However, it's not an entirely accurate answer. I left the church when I was twenty-three because, while working in the Catholic left,

I had encountered a group of women who took the passion for justice I first felt in 1967 and translated it into a concern that affected me directly. It was 1979. I was working for the farmworkers, spending my spare time worrying about Nicaragua, living in a Jesuit-affiliated intentional community in Detroit. But I had begun to drift away from these Catholic issues toward a liberation closer to home.

The women I met then were part of the nascent Reproductive Rights National Network. I was attracted to them because they spoke frankly about things that had been keeping me awake at night. While the Catholic left could speak eloquently about political and social justice, they were mostly silent on any subject that had sexual implications. Meanwhile, I had my first steady male sex partner that year, and was concerned about an array of worries, many of which, for me, didn't even have names. These feminists spoke openly about pregnancy, birth control, abortion, funding for poor women, female orgasm, sexual responsibilities, and other concerns that had entered my bedroom and hit close to my heart. For the first time, liberation had become something that could happen to me.

THE REPRODUCTIVE RIGHTS MOVEMENT emerged from coalitions built between two groups who were dissatisfied with the political tactics of the pro-choice movement: the women's health movement and the new left of the mid 1970s. Both of these factions felt that focusing solely on the legality of abortion would not address the wider concerns associated with women's overall health and material liberation.

One of the first reproductive rights organizations to form was the Reproductive Rights National Network (R2N2), which began in the Midwest in 1978 as an offshoot of the feminist-socialist New American Movement. The organization attempted to connect local activists working on reproductive issues, such as abortion funding and sterilization abuse.[1] R2N2 officially broke from NAM in the spring of 1979 in order to organize more aggressively in areas of women's health. Meanwhile, on the East Coast, the Committee for Abortion Rights and against Sterilization Abuse (CARASA) formed in reaction to the 1977 Supreme Court ruling that permitted state bans on Medicaid funding of abortions. R2N2 and CARASA became the life-blood of the reproductive rights movement and generated the ideology that challenged the hegemony of pro-choice with feminist abortion activism. As Marilyn Katz, founder of R2N2, stated it, "the real impetus for the network was to reframe the debate, to talk about the conditions which would be necessary for women to be able to make a real choice [about whether or not to have children]."[2]

These organizations claimed for women not only the right to legal abortion, but also the rights to childcare, health care, an adequate income, birth control, disability pay during pregnancy for working women, and the right to be protected against unwanted sterilization. Their agenda recognized that granting women the right to an abortion was not a full solution to the problems and injustices associated with reproduction. Many aspects of the social structure needed to be reorganized in order for women to exercise autonomy in the reproductive realm, these feminists argued, and any political strategy that did not attend to these structural needs was inadequate. As Rosalyn Baxandall wrote,

> the right to choose ignores the essential feminist truth that in a male supremacist society no choice a woman makes is entirely free or entirely in her interest. Many women have had abortions they didn't want or wouldn't have wanted if they had plausible means of caring for a child. Countless others would not have gotten pregnant in the first place were it not for inadequate contraception, sexual confusion and guilt, male pressure and other stigmata of female powerlessness.[3]

Or as Marlene Gerber Fried more succinctly claimed, "the decision to fight for choice rather than justice is itself a decision to appeal to those who already have choices."[4] For reproductive rights workers, then, the right to self-determination was inextricably intertwined with material realities; women would be liberated not by the abstract right to an abortion but by the material conditions by which women can choose the course of their own reproductive lives.

These criticisms of pro-choice were persuasive to many of us entering the movement.[5] First of all, reproductive rights activists took issue with pro-choice's appropriation and use of "privacy." As Rhonda Copeland argued, "privacy buttresses the conservative idea that the personal is separate from the political, and that the larger social structure has no impact on private, individual choice. The privacy framework assumes that the society bears no affirmative responsibility for individual choice or action."[6] The pro-choice movement—following the lead set out in *Roe v. Wade* and consistent with the liberal ideology discussed in chapter 1—aggressively and consistently argued that abortion was a private matter, not a subject for public debate at all. Many reproductive rights workers noted that the privacy argument relied on the notion that the state did not have dominion over what happened in the private sphere of the home; this reasoning would permit the state not to provide childcare, prenatal health care, or abortions for poor women. Moreover, reproductive rights workers argued that this sense of privacy had historically been used to reinforce male dominance, even to the point of domestic abuse.

On a related level, the pro-choice movement was criticized for its hierarchical model of organizing. As I suggested in chapter 4, the pro-choice movement attracted large numbers of women who had little background or interest in radical politics. Their lack of political experience limited the pro-choice movement to working within established means—such as legislation—to keep abortion legal. Many pro-choice feminists had neither the time nor inclination to learn or execute the campaigns, movements, and demonstrations that reproductive rights workers believed would effect larger change. Furthermore, because pro-choice feminism was targeted toward women with little time for organizing, the vast majority of women involved in pro-choice politics relied on a small number of full-time, paid, professional staff to inform them on the issues and guide their voting behavior. The lack of political participation beyond financial contribution, isolated pro-choice supporters both from each other and from those in power within the organization.

A third criticism argued that because "pro-choice" had been founded as a direct rebuttal to "pro-life," the pro-choice agenda took up only defensive postures. The reproductive rights workers claimed that with its singular focus on protecting *Roe,* the pro-choice movement could only respond to public and legislative aggressions challenging the lawfulness of the decision. A defensive position was less than desirable because feminism might then be forced into a position of making compromises. And what was often compromised was the reproductive rights of the poor and powerless, such as Medicaid funding for abortions. As Marlene Fried explained,

> this defensive stance implies that we will settle for less . . . going for what we think we can get right now helps to legitimate the view that there are morally acceptable and morally unacceptable abortions and that those decisions are best made by someone other than the pregnant women. Feminists need to be arguing for the right of every woman to make her own decision.[7]

The reproductive rights activists argued for a more proactive political style which would aggressively seek to supply every woman with the material basis she needed to decide her own reproductive future.

For them, compromising the reproductive health of poor women was unacceptable.

Reproductive rights feminists also noted that by focusing solely on the issue of legal abortion, the pro-choice movement had alienated many women. For example, the pro-choice movement was overwhelmingly white and was largely unable to organize women of color. In part this was due to the fact that a "woman's right to choose" does not address the economic constraints that might prevent a woman from obtaining a legal abortion: tactics such as raising prices for abortions, reducing public and private funding, and moving clinics to safer or less conspicuous settings often made it more difficult for women with limited resources to receive abortions. Furthermore, reproductive rights workers argued that access to abortion wasn't the only thing that many women of color needed; they also needed safe and healthy environments in order to choose to carry a pregnancy to term.[8]

Reproductive rights workers advocated that abortion must not only be legal, it must be safe and available to all women. They argued that abortion is not a real "choice" until the social conditions exist wherein a woman can realistically make a different choice. Their work, then, aimed to provide every woman with the housing, food, job, and medical attention she needed in order to have a baby if she wanted to. Instead of relying on the privacy argument, reproductive rights workers grounded their political beliefs on the idea that women ought to have the material basis to make healthy reproductive choices. Instead of being composed of financial contributors, the ranks of the reproductive rights movement included feminists who worked (in many cases, full time) for frontline community organizations, women's health clinics, and socialist groups. Instead of being hierarchical, the reproductive rights organizations were run collectively, without a central core of authority. Instead of focusing on legal issues, the movement attempted to provide a broad range of services and actions for wide-scale social change. Instead of defending abortion rights, the reproductive rights movement attempted to strive for a world where all women could have full control over their bodies.

Rosalind Pollack Petchesky is considered by many to be the major theorist for the reproductive rights movement; her work thus warrants attention here as we look at the theoretical underpinnings of reproductive rights. Petchesky begins with the premise that abortion and other issues associated with reproduction and sexuality are socially and politically organized, that "control over fertility is a matter not only of technology but of the total arrangement of power in society."[9] For Petchesky, childbirth and childcare are not simple biological events; rather they are mediated by many social and political conditions. As she argues, "How, when, and whether to have a child involve different issues for women than for men; yet they do so in ways that vary depending on a woman's class, age, and occupation, as well as the time and culture in which she lives."[10] Thus, because race and social class often influence whether a woman will abort, carry, or conceive in the first place, Petchesky includes these issues as part of her analysis of abortion. She notes that class and racial prejudices, because they affect the material conditions of many women, affect and limit their reproductive options. In short, Petchesky connects reproductive freedom to larger social issues. She points out that the path to every abortion is defined by material conditions which suggest or even dictate the parameters of sexual intercourse, the acceptability of children, and expectations about childcare. Unequal access to abortion and birth control perpetuates existing systems of discrimination. Dealing with the issue of abortion means dealing with these larger injustices.

According to Petchesky, reproductive freedom also demands a redistribution of the responsibilities associated with sex, such as birth control, as well as a reorganization of the roles and tasks associated with childrearing. As she claims, "a materialist (and feminist) view looks forward to an eventual transcendence of the existing social relations of reproduction so that gender is not ultimately the determinant of responsibility. This implies that society be transformed so that men, or society itself, bear an equal responsibility for nurturance and child-care."[11] Thus, she advocates a model in which both men and society participate in the reproductive and childrearing processes; abortion, birth control, and childcare must be the concern of all.

As Petchesky sees it, the state currently operates not to assist women in the reproductive choices they make, but simply to regulate reproduction.[12] In her view, the state intervenes for or against abortion only in order to readjust and perpetuate an economic, social, and gendered system; abortion becomes legal, then, because the larger political system needs to control the number of certain kinds of births, not because society respects women's lives. Women's choices are never seriously entertained; rather, the state attempts to manipulate these choices in order to bring about the desired ends. As Petchesky states, "these policies take different forms for women of different classes, yet the denial that any women should be the final arbiters for their relation to motherhood and their sexuality clearly underlies all [regulatory] policies, whatever their class and racial dimensions."[13] According to Petchesky, *Roe v. Wade* does not contradict this logic because the ruling represented a response to changes in the workforce and in the general population rather than a real step toward women's liberation.[14] Petchesky argues that the state needs to alter its legislative practices and orientations to focus on the lives and needs of women in order that all women can be free to make the choice between bearing a child or not.

Yet she also warns that allowing the state to support children does put women's control over their own bodies at risk. That is, when the state is involved in reproductive decisions, what begins as assistance to women often leads to control. And as Petchesky questions, "Can we really imagine the social conditions in which we would be ready to renounce control over our bodies and reproductive lives—to give over the decision as to whether, when, and with whom we will bear children to the 'community as a whole'?"[15] Thus, she advocates state involvement only to the point where such involvement conflicts with women's choices about their own reproductive desires: "we have to struggle for a society in which responsibility for contraception, pro-creation, and childrearing is no longer relegated to women primarily; and, at the same time, we have to defend the principle of control over our bodies and our reproductive capacities."[16] Thus, although she rejects the liberal notion of abstract "choice" in favor of a socially and historically grounded concept of reproductive freedom, she never surrenders a woman's right to decide the fate of her body. Even if the objective conditions that now constrain women from bearing the children they conceive disappear, and even if a given community is willing to provide childcare and other support services, Petchesky argues that all women still need access to safe abortions. Because pregnancy takes place within the body of a woman, feminists must work both to improve the support structures surrounding women and to make sure that abortion remains (or becomes) available. Although such a balance might be difficult to maintain, Petchesky argues it is necessary for women's liberation.

Petchesky's work is important because she recognizes that positing abortion as totally within the domain of women's decisions is often wrongly translated in today's discourse into the idea that the state has no responsibilities. Petchesky and reproductive rights workers across the country criticized the pro-choice movement for assuming that as long as the abstract "right to choose" is in place, the government or men need not—indeed, should not—involve themselves in the personal choices that women make. Petchesky shows that this attitude toward abortion gets men and the state off the hook, and that while women need to be able to obtain safe abortions, we also need the involvement of men and society to make those abortions (or alternatively the birth and childrearing) materially possible.

IN HER HISTORY OF THE ABORTION MOVEMENT in the United States, Suzanne Staggenborg attributes the breakup of R2N2, CARASA, and other reproductive rights organizations in the early 1990s to several factors. First, the reproductive rights activists had a difficult time gaining a foothold in the dominant, narrowly defined, pro-choice movement because they lacked adequate and stable leadership and financial support. Second, involvement in the reproductive rights movement required a greater commitment of time and energy than pro-choice involvement did, a fact that blocked a large number of women from joining. Finally, many reproductive rights workers found it difficult to implement the multi-issue agendas upon which the organization was founded; energy was divided between a range of issues rather than focused intensely on one action. In short, from Staggenborg's perspective, the reproductive rights organizations failed because the pro-choice movement had more money, support, connections, leadership, and know-how.[17]

These organizations also failed, I suggest, because Americans in general found their arguments unpersuasive. Reproductive rights organizations argued that material conditions must be taken into account when evaluating the morality of abortion, that some women have no choice about reproduction, either because they cannot afford to get an abortion or because they can't afford not to.[18] These arguments never took hold in the larger American public because an individual's right to abortion was seen as unrelated to her material or social status. This is the case, I suggest, because rights language—as it is used in America today—was constructed by and for a white, propertied, male population that was largely unconcerned with material conditions. The liberal convictions that underpin the pro-choice movement reflect the same philosophical principles that were once used to grant rights only to men of the upper classes. The pro-choice movement (and consequently many feminists in America) view the historical roots of these liberal principles as unproblematic and use the principles to address the issues surrounding women and reproduction. The concerns set forth by reproductive rights workers were dismissed because they challenged the liberal foundations upon which America was built.

Stated differently, the language and strategies of the pro-choice movement are hegemonic today because Americans believe that the abstract idea of personal choice is of primary importance, even when one's material conditions make choices impossible. "Pro-choice" is a convincing argument because it resonates with the liberal, individualist consciousness of a majority of Americans today; what we do with our private lives—which includes reproduction and abortion—should not be subject to state intervention. However, I suggest that the political framework that stands behind "a woman's right to choose" is inadequate, not only because it is built on a philosophical system which has historically excluded women, but because in today's abortion debates, it often works to oppress women further.[19] Just as the ostensibly neutral ideology functions to favor rationality in the private domain of reproduction, it also functions to benefit those already in power when it comes to abortion in general.

Before showing why this is true, it is important to recognize that the liberal framework from which the pro-choice logic emerged has historically worked to benefit many women. Political theorists such as Mary Wollstonecraft, Margaret Fuller, Elizabeth Cady Stanton, Harriet Taylor, and John Stuart Mill successfully argued for women's liberation based on the principles of liberalism, gaining for women the rights to vote, to education, to due process under law, and to economic independence. But in what follows, I focus on the limitations of a politics based solely on liberal principles for the issue of abortion today. While we need not renounce the work that has been done within liberal structures that have given us voice and freedom, we must develop a vision that transcends the drawbacks of a liberal foundation. As Zillah Eisenstein has written, "as long as the liberalism in feminism parades invisibly, it cannot be assessed as contradictory with feminism, nor can dimensions of it be self-consciously reworked."[20] By examining the biases contained in the liberal construction of selfhood and reproduction, we can develop agendas which address the material and social concerns associated with abortion.

As I articulated in chapter 1, liberal theory presumes that human individuals ontologically precede culture; that is, the essential characteristics of human beings, which cluster around the attribute of reason, exist prior to and independent of social order. Moreover, liberalism insists that we are born free of particularities, except for the common human trait of rationality. Specifically, we lack convictions about what constitutes human good, convictions which might mark one as different or nonrational. What makes a liberal society work is not the particular telos or purpose or end at which it aims, but precisely its refusal to choose in advance among competing purposes and ends. The society is just because it allows each of us to choose our own good; what makes one just in this society is therefore not the good one chooses, but simply one's capacity to make such choices. But although liberalism appears to accommodate differing and competing convictions about the good, upon closer examination it becomes clear that those competing convictions may never override or take precedence over the public commitment that each person should be allowed to choose his or her own good.

I suggest that whether or not a woman can in reality obtain an abortion is not an issue for liberal society. The right to an abortion is granted to an abstracted person, one unencumbered by poverty or isolation. The only significant factor is that women have the abstract ability to choose abortion. We are allowed to be concerned with how pregnancy and reproduction affect particular women only as long as we do so in private spaces, and only as long as our commitment to something like feminism doesn't interfere with our prior (more important) commitment to keep such particularities out of public, political space.

Moreover, I suggest that the unencumbered nature of the abstract, public individual often renders that individual more competitive in daily life. The liberal subject is available to work long hours, to relocate, to make a complete commitment to the career that will eventually define identity. In such a climate, anything that restricts the individual's ability to compete—such as pregnancy—can only be understood as a drawback, as something to be overcome. The abstract right to abortion offers the pregnant woman the option of regaining her nonpregnant status in order to fully and competitively participate in the public sphere. Abortion thus functions as an equalizer; any woman who does not want a pregnancy can simply have it removed and thus immediately return herself to the Ur-position of the abstracted liberal self. The idea that pregnant women might desire more choices than "being pregnant" or "not being pregnant"—such as more adequate childcare or larger systems of kinship, in which the cost and burden of raising a child is spread among many—is beyond the limits of the liberal imagination.

In my thinking, it is not a coincidence that the abstracted, competitive, nonpregnant person of the public sphere most resembles men. In constructing this political environment solely out of their own imaginations, men viewed their circumstances as the central defining experiences of individuality. In the liberal system, then, legalized abortion offers women the choice to be either like men (not pregnant) or different from men (pregnant). Those people who occupy the public realm of citizenship, who, as Michael Warner expresses it, "transcend the given realities of their bodies and their status," are "implicitly, even explicitly, white, male, literate, and propertied." Those who are not white, male, literate, and propertied, although they are "tolerated," continuously display what Warner calls "the humiliating positivity of the particular," and are thus specified as "less than public."[21] Women, as a result of the way that reproduction is structured, are often encumbered with the humiliating positivity of pregnancy, which is to say that as a result of pregnancy, they are less than perfect citizens in liberal society.

In liberal society, if a person forgoes abortion and "chooses" pregnancy, the state assumes that this person alone will take responsibility for this choice and for the child, with little support from society at large. The choice of whether or not to have children is seen as a private choice, no different than the other choices made in the private sphere, such as what one eats, where one lives, or what kind of car one buys. The liberal state does not and cannot offer support for raising children if it doesn't offer reciprocal support for many other private choices.[22] Liberalism rests on the assumption that we are all equal and unencumbered to begin with and that we are all similarly placed in relation to the benefits society has to offer. This presumption of individual equality not only masks major differences in access to power and resources, it also disregards the material needs associated with reproduction. The meaning of "choice" (as in pro-choice) in a society where women as a group have less power than men and where certain classes of women have even less than others must be challenged. Women, by virtue of the fact that they are assigned the role of mothers and caretakers, very often do not have the freedom to pursue the benefits encoded in liberal society.

In liberal society, public life is formulated as wholly different from private. The postindustrial nineteenth-century American ideology of the Cult of Domesticity defined these two realms as necessarily separate and entirely gendered: men were associated with public life, business, and industry; women with keeping the home and raising children.[23] Thus, by structuring life into these two realms, men retained economic control of their families while wives reproduced the "haven in a heartless world" for their men to return home to. For more than a century, academic political and historical analysis focused solely on the public, economic sphere and overlooked the activities of the home. Liberal feminists involved in pro-choice politics perpetuate this bifurcation by arguing that abortion is necessary because it is a matter of privacy. In doing so, they inadvertently reinscribe women back into a system that assigns our work in accordance with how biological function is understood and constructed. The appeal to the private sphere for protection makes it virtually impossible for all but the wealthiest women (that is, if they are wealthy enough to hire service and childcare workers) to escape the oppressions associated with that sphere. Although the legalization of abortion is meant to enable women to enter the public sphere on an equal basis, I suggest that women will not be released from their obligations in the private sphere until the sphere of privacy no longer exists. As long as the world is conceptualized as divided between home and work, most women will have the responsibility for their homes, and often for other women's homes as well. Legal access to abortion alone will not change this.

Because liberalism separates public life from private and then assigns membership and duties on the basis of gender, it is a system which finally works to the service of men. The separation of life into two spheres is not "natural" but is itself a way of constructing gender. Women's roles as mothers, caregivers, homemakers are constantly organized and constructed by society. Moreover, those assigned to the public sphere are freed from childrearing and domestic tasks in order to pursue careers and professional identities. A feminist position which relies on this bifurcated system for protection and freedom is shortsighted and inadequate.

The appeal to privacy as a way of protecting women also serves to increase both isolation and oppression. Issues that are private are issues not to be discussed. Labeling abortion private functions to keep women isolated from one another, to keep us from discovering our collective best interests, to convince us that we're happy in that isolation. When the right to privacy is invoked, although it is intended to protect us from state intervention, it also functions to protect us from each other. *Roe v. Wade* did not contradict this strategy of isolation; indeed, the legislation ignored feminist demands for absolute reproductive freedom in favor of a controlled freedom that was limited by the extent of the right to privacy. The pro-choice movement extends the isolation not only by continually appealing to privacy as the governing right involved in abortion, but also by operating in a manner that discourages "members" from meeting each other.

The use of privacy has another flaw; it is founded on the false presumption that people will treat each other fairly in the home.[24] The incidence of domestic violence and child abuse points out, I believe, that some men who are trained and encouraged to be competitive and aggressive during the day find it hard to turn those dispositions off at night.[25] The field of sexual intercourse, although "protected" by one's right to privacy, thus often becomes a battleground. The protection of abortion and sexuality under the rubric of privacy often serves to support men's sexual demands on and abuses of women.

Similarly, the foundation of privacy has reinforced the American desire to "keep the government out of personal business," an atmosphere which eventually led to the *Webster v. Reproductive Health Services* decision. "Webster" was William Webster, Missouri's attorney general, who had defended the 1986 state statute that banned the use of public facilities and employees for abortions. The Supreme Court ruled in favor of Webster and declared that although the government would allow abortion, no public money (and no hospital or health care provider who received public money) could be used to support abortion. This decision verified the idea that the government would no longer support women's "private" needs for abortion with "public" funds. In other words, the government had given women the right to choose an abortion if they could afford one but, as a result of Webster, had no obligation to provide them with anything else. As Katharine Bartlett and Roseanne Kennedy explain,

> Grounding the right [to abortion] in privacy . . . permitted the Supreme Court to limit access to abortion by poor women and, further, reinforced the ideology that dominance and abuse within the "private" family are beyond the law's authority. This [has] taught feminists that a strategy of piecemeal reform often reinforces rather than weakens the institutional foundations of gender hierarchy, and that winning now frequently means a loss somewhere down the line.[26]

Liberalism views men and women as participants in competing spheres, or as Wendy Williams puts it, "on different life tracks." As Williams claims, "that fundamentally dichotomous view which characterized men as breadwinner, women as homemaker-childrearer, foreclosed the possibility that the courts could successfully apply an equality model to the sexes."[27] Contemporary abortion laws allow women to be more competitive in the public sphere but do not challenge the fundamental associations between women and home, and between men and work. Moreover, although its aim is to bring about equality, the legal right to abortion reinscribes the idea that women are different, that they need "special rights" such as abortion in order to compete in public life successfully. This mark of difference virtually secures women's oppression over the long run. Every time abortion is invoked inside the liberal system, it serves as a reminder that women are not ideal, unencumbered, subjects. It serves as a reminder that women are not like men.[28]

SEVERAL RECENT WORKS IN FEMINIST THEORY propose ways of viewing human liberation outside the frame of liberalism. These works, I believe, address some of the problems associated with pro-choice politics that I have highlighted here. In keeping with new developments in feminist theory, I suggest that we need to think about the human subject in terms of the practices and social orientations of those individuals not adequately represented by the liberal subject. These new works in feminist theory point to the work of Carol Gilligan's *In a Different Voice* as a new alternative model of subjectivity. I offer here a summary of Gilligan's findings, then, because I believe they offer a methodological alternative to the ethics promulgated by the liberal, unencumbered subject.

In comparing the ethical responses and judgments of young men and women, Gilligan argued that every moral problem could be viewed through either an ethic of justice or an ethic of care. These two orientations are not themselves moral principles or rational guidelines, but rather constitute "different ways of viewing the world that organize both thinking and feeling."[29] Gilligan demonstrated these differences by giving her adolescent subjects a test of moral reasoning. Lawrence Kohlberg's well-known scenario describes a man named Heinz, who is considering whether to steal a drug he cannot afford in order to save the life of his wife. In Gilligan's research, most of her male subjects adopted a justice orientation suggesting that Heinz should steal the drug. According to Gilligan, the dilemma was construed by young men as a conflict between the values of property and life. Allegiance to life should win out, as one eleven-year-old boy claimed, because "a human life is worth more than money, and if the druggist only makes $1,000, he is still going to live, but if Heinz doesn't steal the drug, his wife is going to die." In this justice-oriented response, as Gilligan suggests, morality is evaluated with "mathematical precision."[30]

In contrast, the response of young girls of the same age, according to Gilligan, "considers neither property nor law but rather the effect that theft could have on the relationship between Heinz and his wife. As the eleven-year-old girl sees it, "If he stole the drug, he might save his wife then, but if he did, he might have to go to jail, and then his wife might get sicker again, and he couldn't get more of the drug, and it might not be good. So, they really should just talk it out and find some other way to make the money."[31] Gilligan argues that this female response "sees in the dilemma not a math problem with humans but a narrative of relationships that extends over time." The young girl, "sees the [case] as a mistake, believing that the world should just share things more and then people wouldn't have to steal." In Gilligan's analysis, the caring ethic was not a principle but an activity, a way of being attentive to connections, influences, and relationships as part of moral discernment.[32]

Through a series of interviews with a wider population of adults, Gilligan found that those who relied completely on an abstract sense of justice to guide their moral behavior had difficulty making exceptions, and that their abstractions often led to their own isolation and dissatisfaction. On the other hand, she found that those women who relied solely on the ethic of care most often found themselves in limited and unfulfilled roles; they often functioned as little more than caretakers, having no "selves" of their own. Thus, Gilligan advocated a third type of moral development in which both men and women see the importance and interconnection of care and justice.[33] Here, individuals take specific contexts as well as moral rules and maxims into account when making decisions and judgments. The synthesis between these two voices aims to discredit the abstract conception of morality underpinning rights language; at the same time, it suggests that caring should always occur within value-driven systems. As Elizabeth Schneider sees it, "Gilligan imagines that this third stage of development will be based upon the synthesis of male and female voices—those of rights and responsibilities. The discourse is no longer either simply about justice or simply about caring; rather it is about bringing them together to transform the domain."[34] I stand in agreement that both voices are needed to achieve an ethic that attends to nurturance, compassion, responsibility, attentiveness. Both are needed to bring an end to injustice and oppression in the lives of real women. Both are needed to form the foundation of feminist ethics.[35]

Gilligan's work has been appropriated and criticized by feminists of many persuasions. Some feminists have used her data to suggest that, as a result of their natural orientation toward care, women are inherently morally superior to men.[36] Others argue that Gilligan's work—and those who support it—make essentialist claims that ultimately serve to confine women to the domestic sphere. These feminists argue that the public sphere, and the justice associated with it, are the sources and locations of power in society; all feminists, they say, should not try to theorize their oppression as somehow wielding power, but should instead be working to secure the power of the public for themselves.[37] I agree with Joan Tronto, however, that interpreting Gilligan's work as describing or prescribing a moral code particular to women misses the mark. Gilligan's work is interesting not because of what it tells us about women, but rather because of its significance for contemporary moral theory. We do not need to understand the voices of justice and care as essentially connected to gender, Tronto argues, in order to use both aspects of moral decision making to formulate an ethical methodology that is both justice and care oriented.[38]

In a similar fashion, Seyla Benhabib focuses on an ethic of justice *and* care as a way out of the problems associated with the abstract liberal subject. For her, the importance of Gilligan's work is not that it offers empirical claims about women's unique moral voice; rather, she sees Gilligan's combined ethic as an "anticipatory utopian critique," a claim about the ways we ought to be relating to each other.[39] This ethic locates the ideal human subject—that is to say, every human subject—within a web of social and economic constraints and possibilities. Benhabib advocates a move from the "generalized other" (who is both historically and imaginatively male) to the "concrete other"—a move that "requires us to view each and every rational being as an individual with a concrete history, identity and affective emotional constitution."[40]

In short, many feminist theorists today suggest that we use Gilligan's insights to reconstruct moral inquiry in a way that includes systems of caring as well as principles of justice. This prescription recognizes that ethical methods are not determined by gender. Everyone has the potential to employ both care and justice; one's orientation toward one or the other is a result of cultural training rather than nature. Thus, an ethic of justice and care can also help us overcome gender differentiation. In my opinion, this combined ethic offers new insight and methodology for dealing with the conflicted issue of abortion.

Precisely what are justice and care, and how do they interact and relate? To my thinking, justice means a belief in the idea that following moral principles can help us attain a good and rewarding life. We cannot just act as we want (emotivism); nor does staying within the limits of human law necessarily lead to happiness and fulfillment. Rather, we need principles to help us organize and evaluate the world around us and to guide our actions.[41] Caring, to me, means that we understand that these principles and the beliefs that hold them only exist within a specific, historical context, a context which is itself worthy of attention and may at certain times override or revise the intent of the principle. Attention to this context means examining and evaluating how an act will change or affect the world around us.[42]

A simple example: I am, at the time of this writing, in the job market for a full-time academic position. My colleagues encourage me to "take the best job I get," a justice-based principle which operates widely throughout the academic profession. However, I have a family—including a ten-year-old daughter—that needs to be considered in the decision-making process. Am I willing to move us all for a job I'm not sure I'll like? Am I willing to resign all of us to a long and exhausting commute in order to take the best job? Am I willing to see my family only once or twice a month for it? An ethic of justice and care implies that my definition of "the best job I get" will be bound by what I and my family feel we can or want to endure. The act of caring means figuring others into the equation itself, not as an add-on or afterthought. Rather than making a decision about "the best job" and trying to accommodate my family after the fact, my family is factored into the evaluation of the job itself.

In advocating an ethical methodology that combines justice and care, I suggest that we recognize that our principles of fairness, of what is right and wrong, exist within a world of contingent and contextual lives. I do not intend simply to invert the public/private hierarchical paradigm by valorizing the private; it's not enough just to care without recognizing the principles and beliefs which operate as moral guideposts in every situation. Rather, it is my intention to subvert the separation by acknowledging that neither justice nor care works or makes sense alone. I propose to collapse these two orientations into one ethical methodology that could form the foundation for feminism, a foundation which challenges the bifurcation of public life from private and claims that both women and men ought to have the options of living full, satisfying lives both at home and at work.[43]

I offer the following statements as a starting point for a feminist ethic of care and justice in relation to abortion: I believe that no woman ought to bear a child against her will. I also believe, as a corollary, that no woman ought to be forced into having an abortion (or a sterilization) because she cannot organize enough social and economic resources to have her baby. If we use these two principles as guideposts while attending to concrete contexts, the politics of abortion becomes much more coherent. A combined ethic of justice and care means acting out of a much broader range of concerns than the simple conviction that a woman has "a right to choose." That principle alone is not enough; each and every woman exists in a context (sometimes the context of poverty, fear, or hopelessness) that must be addressed in a feminist framework.

Pro-choice feminists might suggest that the common denominator of my two proposed statements is in fact "choice"; in their eyes, each of these statements rearticulates their assertion that women have the right to "choose" to carry a pregnancy to term or not. In that framework, justice is served when abortion is legally available. However, I suggest that when we reread these statements through an ethic that combines justice with care, our political work is a lot harder. Securing a legal right to abortion is not enough; the convictions associated with caring compel us to work for the social, emotional, and material conditions whereby a woman can choose either an abortion or a baby. In order to place power and authority back in the hands of women, we must work to make abortions available to all women, regardless of poverty, inconvenience, or isolation. We must also work to provide women with adequate resources and circumstances so that she may have that baby if she chooses. We must consider not only the abstract principles, but the specific contexts in which those principles are operating.

In every unwanted pregnancy, a particular woman exists in a web of responsibilities and options. In an ethic based solely on abstract justice, women with unwanted pregnancies are treated as individuals without histories, without relationships, without contexts. While such women may seek help in having a baby rather than an abortion, a justice-based ethic implies it is sufficient to grant her the right to abort. A woman with an unwanted pregnancy may be crying out for guidance, for help in coping with this financial, physical, and emotional burden, but a justice ethic will instruct us to respect her privacy, individuality, and autonomy by staying out of "her business."

Our job as feminists, I believe, is to make each woman's context part of the moral procedure. Every woman makes her choice in relation to her options; every woman has the right to explore existing options, to try to create new ones, and to discuss and evaluate her choices with those around her. As feminists who opt for a combined ethic of justice and caring in relation to abortion, it is our responsibility to make sure that the necessary options are materially available to her, to make sure that she knows about them, and to make ourselves available for discussion. By allowing ourselves to become part of the decision-making process, we live the activity of caring.

However, a sole focus on caring does not address the political work necessary to keep abortion legal, or the future legislative and organizational work that will make abortion available and safe for all women. As Joan Tronto argues, those who advocate a methodology based completely on caring are "unable to show a convincing way of turning these [caring] virtues into a realistic approach to the kinds of problems that caring will confront in the real world."[44] Our principles are needed as moral guideposts. It is not enough simply to care, we must have beliefs which direct us to move or advise in one direction or another. These beliefs may cause us to go to Washington to bring about change, but a combined ethic of care and justice teaches us that Washington is not the only place that political work happens.

Women need a broader range of options regarding reproduction, and we need support in executing those options; we need systems that allow us to choose to have babies that are "defective" or nonrational; we need social support systems that make it acceptable to have either an abortion or to have a baby and relinquish it for adoption; we need systems which enable us to support the children we have, in which reproduction is viewed as legitimate work and not simply a burden or strain on the state; we need safe and reliable access to abortion and birth control whatever our material base. It is no longer enough for us to use a liberal-based theory to fight for conditions that allow us the abstract right to have abortions, for as Marlene Gerber Fried writes, "counting on the police to keep the clinics open, counting on the courts to preserve abortion rights, counting on the medical establishment to provide abortion services makes us complicit with an oppressive system, a system which should be challenged, not relied upon."[45]

Our feminist task in relation to abortion is now twofold. First, we must work to provide the social and material conditions which broaden our range of options. Access to childcare, health care, birth control, and freedom from sterilization abuse cannot be treated as separate, unrelated issues. The necessary restructuring will not happen as long as "privacy" is segregated from public life and relegated to a lesser status. Second, in order to escape the problems that accompany liberalism, it is our feminist task to continually retheorize social life, and to generate a system whereby the public and the private become more integrated, less gendered entities. We must not only work to provide women with the necessary material and social conditions to choose either a baby or an abortion; we must also challenge the grounds and assumptions upon which our politics rest.

CHAPTER SIX

Christianity and the Abortion Wars

◄○►

*I didn't talk to one person who felt supported by her church
when it came to dealing with unwanted pregnancy.*

Ann Perkins, *Bitter Fruit*

Across America today, young Christian women who find
themselves with unwanted pregnancies go to their priests or
pastors to discuss their options. Whether the minister is Methodist
or Presbyterian, high church or evangelical, young or old, male or
female, chances are very high that the response and pastoral care will
fall into one of two categories. If he is "pro-choice" (meaning that
personally he believes that every woman has a right to choose what
happens to her own body), he will probably ask the woman what she
wants or what she is called to do in her heart. If she suggests that she
might be considering abortion, the minister might help her find a
clinic, procure the necessary money, and assure her that her choice is
both moral and appropriate. If the minister is, however, "pro-life"
(meaning she is personally against abortion because every fetus has a
right to live), she will probably discourage the woman from having
an abortion, and perhaps, if the woman is willing, help her find a
way to slip out of town for a while into some sort of "situation"
where she can bear the child alone and in peace. Later, the minister
may help to place the baby with an appropriate Christian family.

In both scenarios, the ministers will respect the woman's desire for confidentiality. No questions will be asked about the father; no questions will be asked about the circumstances under which the woman became pregnant. To ask such questions, both ministers would agree, would be to invade this woman's privacy. In either scenario, no one else in the church will likely know that this woman is, or was, pregnant. In both cases, the pregnant woman is treated as an individual without a history, without relationships, without a context. Her decision will be made on what she feels is personally right or wrong for her, or if her minister is able to exert his or her influence, on an abstract principle about when life begins. Both ministers have learned to respect the privacy and integrity of all women, and even if they sense that this particular woman is crying out for support, for guidance, for her loved ones to tell her what to do, each of these ministers can only offer so much and can only push so far before bumping up against her autonomy and individuality.

This chapter is written out of my conviction that the Christian church participates in the creation of a new order and therefore, has the potential for developing alternative methodologies that can overcome the bifurcated abortion debates. Here, I suggest that the language of "pro-life" and "pro-choice" is ultimately injurious to contemporary Christians. In keeping with the larger argument presented in this book, I suggest that as Christians, we need to move beyond the idea that abortion is always right or always wrong. Instead, we need to rely on the resources located in our theologies to articulate a world that transcends this debate and is more faithful to the Christian practices of welcoming the stranger and caring for each other in the community called church. My claims and arguments in this chapter are thus neither ethnographic nor sociological but rather stem from my conviction that the church could be dealing with the issue of abortion in a manner much more harmonious with its tradition.

Stated simply, in treating Christian women with unwanted pregnancies as isolated and abstract individuals, we rob them of their connections, relationships, and community, and we rob ourselves of the opportunity to care for and welcome both them and their children. By making recommendations based on the philosophical maxims we hold about life's beginnings, we overlook those characteristics and practices which have commonly defined all that is good about "church," including both community and hospitality. In relying on pro-life or pro-choice ideology, we are apt to ignore the way this decision will affect both the pregnant woman's life and our communal life together. In what follows, I suggest that the ethical methods of casuistry (presented in chapter 2) and caring (outlined in chapter 5) can both be used by contemporary Christian churches seeking a more faithful response to situations of unwanted pregnancy. I suggest specific ways that can help us shift our thinking from an ethics based on abstract individuals, principles, and laws to a resolution based on a balance between an ethics of justice and an ethics of care. What we can accomplish, I believe, is a way to move beyond the pro-life/pro-choice impasse into a territory where these women, and the communities of which they are part, can function collectively to make the best decision possible for each case.

In chapter 2, I argued that casuistry has had limited success in dealing with the multiple constructions of abortion across communities; I suggested that even this extremely flexible methodology often fails to account for or justify the competing worldviews of American Catholics and traditional Roman Catholics. In this chapter, I revisit casuistry in greater depth because I believe that if we can agree to transcend the bifurcated camps of the current abortion wars, the methodology *can* help us build a more faithful Christian response to the contemporary moral issue of abortion. If proportionalists and proponents of double effect—or Christian pro-choicers and Christian pro-lifers—could agree to suspend their commitments to absolutist rhetoric and to rise above their abstract positions on abortion, casuistry may offer a way to be both flexible and faithful to the tradition. Although casuistry cannot adjudicate between competing communities when those communities construct abortion out of entirely different principles and beginning points, it can help us to think about how the issues surrounding abortion can be dealt with once those abstract principles are laid aside. Thus, although various churches and denominations currently define themselves in relation to abstractions associated with abortion, my argument here is that all Christians should instead revisit their commitment both to communal life in Christ and to welcoming the stranger (hospitality) in order to achieve a more faithful response to the problems associated with unwanted pregnancy. Casuistry serves as an excellent place for those of us inside a disciple community to begin to transcend the schism initiated by pro-life and pro-choice discourses. Coupled with commitments to community and hospitality, casuistry allows us to recover a part of our history that is obscured and lost.

To repeat Jonsen and Toulmin's definition, casuistry is "the analysis of moral issues, using procedures of reasoning based on paradigms and analogies, leading to the formulation of expert opinions about the existence and stringency of particular moral obligations, framed in terms of rules or maxims that are general but not universal or invariable, since they hold good with certainty only in the typical conditions of the agent and circumstances of the action."[1] That is, rather than stating a priori and for every circumstance that abortion is wrong (or right), casuistry recommends that we take each case separately and analyze the morality of the intervention by employing analogies as moral guideposts. For example, when we think about what to do when a store clerk undercharges us, we ask ourselves, "Would keeping the extra money be more like stealing or finding money on the street?" We think about our behavior in relation to other behaviors it resembles. A similar process could happen for each abortion. Does abortion in a particular instance represent an act of caring? a murder? a freeing choice? In using the wisdom of our lives to make decisions, casuistry offers an approach that relies on the context of an act for its moral evaluation. In each case, the conditions that surround the unwanted pregnancy are not factors to be extracted, but rather help to constitute the morality of the act itself.

A casuist today might deliberate on the morality of any abortion not by appealing to principles such as pro-life or pro-choice, but by inquiring about the particular conditions of the case. These conditions, when considered alongside the map of moral intuitions that we inherit as part of our membership in the Christian tradition, can help us to think better about individual cases of abortion in our own churches today. Casuistry will not start a moral inquiry by arguing that abortion, in every case and regardless of circumstances, is always wrong or always right; rather, as we shall see, the moral nature of each abortion depends on a system of real circumstances. The ethical methodology encoded in the practice of casuistry is precisely the kind of method that our churches today—especially those women with unwanted pregnancies who belong to and help constitute our churches—long for and deserve. Casuistry's virtue is that it attends to the context of an act without ignoring individual claims about morality.

As we've discussed, casuistry had its origins in the Roman Catholic practice of periodic and regular confessing of sins that began roughly in the fifth century. Before this practice arose, Christians could only receive formal ecclesial forgiveness once in a lifetime. As Pierre Payer notes,

[Public penance] was a severe practice which could only be undertaken *once* in a lifetime and which carried heavy disabilities. Those who underwent public penance could not marry afterwards if they were single, could not engage in sexual relations during and after public penance if they were already married, could not enter military service, and were barred from becoming clerics in the future. To undergo public penance was a serious decision not to be made lightly.[2]

In response to these harsh strictures, many early Christians waited until the end of their lives to make this public confession. In the meantime, though, many needed to discuss the state of their souls with someone in ecclesial authority in order to better understand when, how, and if they had sinned. Indeed, because penance was available only once, such "private soul-guidance," as John NcNeill notes, "was recommended [by church authorities]."[3] These guidance sessions, some scholars argue, began as a practice primarily in monasteries, where superiors of monastic communities would listen to and comment upon the sins of community members. The practice quickly spread and laypeople from surrounding areas made their way to monasteries, offering to trade much needed material goods for the priests to "hear" their sins. The priest, in this transaction, functioned as an ordained proxy for the entire community and for God and was thus able—following confession—to set the penitent "right" without the harsh penalties of public penance. By the sixth century, regular, private confession had become the norm for most lay Christians, and eventually the practice of nonrepeatable public penance died away.

The casebooks used by the clergy to assign appropriate penances for these confessions did not include ironclad rules, but suggested instead practical categories in relation to particular sins. "Adultery," for example, might have a number of entries in a priest's penitential, such as "for money," "for pleasure," or "for repayment of debt," with commentaries and penances corresponding not only to the sin but

THE LIMITATIONS OF THE CURRENT DEBATE

also to the circumstances. The goal of confession exemplified by these books, and by the practice of casuistry itself, was not to exact a just measure of penance for the sin (as it was assumed, at least early on, that this would be accomplished in the one-time public penance). The point in these activities was pastoral; the confessor's task was to help the penitent to understand the breadth and depth of his or her wrongdoing. To do so, the priest would inquire about the context and circumstances of the action. He was instructed, as Jonsen and Toulmin recount, "to note how long the sinner persisted in the sin, what understanding he has, by what passions he was assailed, how great was his strength and by what oppressions he was driven to his sin."[4] When all of these circumstances were taken into consideration, the priest attempted to match this particular case, analogically and paradigmatically, to others in his penitential and subsequently to assign a proper penance.

For example, in the preface to a penitential attributed to the Venerable Bede (d. 735), one casuist wrote,

> Not all persons are to be weighed in one and the same balance, although they be associated in one fault, but there shall be discrimination for each of these, rich or poor; freeman or slave; small child, boy, youth, young man or old man; stupid or intelligent; layman, cleric or monk; bishop, presbyter, deacon, subdeacon or reader, ordained or unordained; married or unmarried; pilgrim, virgin, canoness, or nuns; the weak, the sick or the well.
> The priest shall make a distinction for the character of the sins or of the men—a continent person or one who is incontinent; for acts performed willfully or by accident; in public or in secret; with what compunction a penitent makes amends; under compulsion or voluntarily; the time and place of the fault, and so on.[5]

Attention to such details, I suggest, functioned to help the confessor keep rules, principles, and maxims in balance with the particularities of each case. While the priest was not at liberty to disregard the moral framework that he had inherited, he was free to interpret it in relation to a wide circle of circumstances and events surrounding the case. He was free, as one casuist articulated it, to "grasp the equity of the case from the circumstances."[6] In casuistrical practice, universal and invariable principles were held in check by the consideration of circumstances.

While the earliest penitential books "rarely went beyond the citing of a scriptural or patristic text to justify the penitential verdict," by the twelfth century, casuistry had become a full-blown scholarly endeavor entailing attention not only to the sin committed but to the way the sin was described, the conditions of the commission, and the character and position of the agent.[7] The later manuals reflected the complexities that arose when differing circumstances surrounded what had previously appeared to be the same sin. However, by about 1,000 C.E., casuistry had become so infused with Roman and canon law that more attention was paid to the intricacies of each abstract case than to the circumstances and spiritual condition of the penitent. That is, while the details of the cases became more and more specific, the penitential books themselves became more and more lawlike. Indeed, in the hands of the law-loving Jesuits, casuistry took on almost mathematical precision and certainty. What was originally intended to perform the tasks of alleviating the Christian's conscience and standing in for the entire worshiping community in the enactment of the Christian promise of forgiveness, became, by the High Middle Ages, little more than a legalistic exacting of penance. In this shift, significant aspects of the earlier confessional practices were lost.

Some of the redeeming aspects that were lost in this shift have surfaced again, I suggest, in Carol Gilligan's work on morality and gender discussed in chapter 5. The balance that Gilligan seeks between care and justice resembles the way that priests dealt with their parishioners in the early confessionals. The priest was able to treat his penitents with both caring and justice, taking into consideration their individual circumstances without losing sight of their shared inherited principles and maxims. Rules were indeed important, but care for the spiritual and emotional life of his parishioners was every priest's highest concern. Both the casuists and the care ethicists, in their attempt to achieve such balance, offer us rich models for thinking ethically about the problems of abortion our churches face today.

The similarities between Gilligan's work and the methodological assumptions made by the early priests in the first confessionals can be instructive in our attempt to appropriate this balanced method in our churches today. Both Gilligan and the casuists assume that the moral self is radically situated and particularized. As Lawrence Blum argues regarding Gilligan,

> [The moral self] is "thick" rather than "thin," defined by its historical connections and relationships. . . . For Gilligan, care morality is about the particular agent's caring for and about the particular friend or child with whom she has come to have this particular relationship. Morality is not only about how the impersonal "one" is meant to act toward the impersonal "other."[8]

The same is true, I hold, for the early confessionals. Moral discernment in the casuistrical tradition is concerned with relationships and circumstances. Neither the penitent nor the wronged person can be abstracted or generalized in the confessional; indeed, the act of confession, especially in the early church, was constituted by the discernment of particulars. Morality, both in the confessional and in an ethics of care, is not a matter of the individual's obeying abstract laws or principles; rather, in both programs, each person is seen, as Blum suggests of Gilligan, "as approaching the world of action bound by ties and relationships (friend, colleague, parent, child) which confront her as, at least to some extent, givens."[9]

As the late medieval moralists became more and more absorbed in articulating precise, legal cases in the penitentials, the practice of the confessional shifted, in Gilligan's terms, from an ethical system based on a balance between justice and care to one that was totally invested in a law-based sense of justice. By the sixteenth century, casuistry was faltering because scholastic morality, like Gilligan's "male" justice, had begun to be calculated on mathematical and deductive bases. That is, morality became a matter of following the letter of the law. By the end of the seventeenth century, casuistry had virtually disappeared precisely because it had overemphasized an ethic of legalized justice and drifted away from the relationships, connections, and circumstances incumbent on each individual case.

As Jonsen and Toulmin's book signifies, however, the casuistrical method is once again under consideration among moral theologians, moral philosophers, and Christian ethicists alike. Similar concerns regarding relationality and justice are appearing in the apparently unrelated fields of feminist theory, philosophical ethics, and developmental psychology. As I see it, we live today in a world where too much emphasis is placed on abstract and deductive argumentation, and not enough of our moral lives go into examining the contexts and relationships which surround our ethical decisions. While in some cases, it is easy to understand a principle as being embedded within a circumstance (for example, our willingness to "lie" or "bend the truth" to a person on the verge of suicide), we are unable for the most part to view abortions contextually. The discourses of caring and casuistry demonstrate that context must be routinely integrated into abstraction, that care is part of what justice means. Nowhere are these discourses more necessary than in the current debate over abortion.

In what remains here, then, I try to lay out some practical implications for a church committed to overcoming the abstractions "pro-life" and "pro-choice" in favor of the more historical and traditional practices of community and hospitality. First, no woman creates a baby by herself; even if she is completely isolated in this world, at least one other person participated in this act. Understanding that the politics surrounding sexual intercourse can be extremely complicated and painful, Christian ministers very often do not ask too many questions about the father. It's not our business, we tell ourselves; and if the woman reports that the father "isn't in the picture," we don't push further. I suggest, however, that getting the father involved should indeed be the first concern. Many feminist authors writing about abortion decry the state of affairs where a man gets a woman pregnant and then just walks away. They point out that "a woman's right to choose" all too often becomes "a man's right to use." In the Christian church, this is unacceptable. If two people were to receive an award or had committed a crime, it would be neither fair nor honest to honor or punish only one. Before anything else, therefore, the church should attempt to remedy those situations where unwanted pregnancy is addressed only as a woman's private problem. Furthermore, because the Christian church has an existing network for thinking and teaching about ethical behavior, it has the potential to become a model community for holding men responsible for their part in the reproductive act.

Thus, when a woman comes to a minister for help or guidance with her unwanted pregnancy, that minister must inquire about the father. Our pastors should be taught in seminary that it is their responsibility to bring the man into the situation, unless doing so would bring harm to the woman. If the man is a member of any other Christian church, his pastor should be contacted and both should be invited to and encouraged to attend a discussion. By training our future ministers to respond in this way, the church could, in not too much time, significantly change the script in which abortion is chosen simply for the convenience of the man.[10]

Although this suggestion to alter the way that men are involved in reproduction might seem hard to implement, I suggest that it is very possible as long as the church continues to train people for the Christian ministry in centralized locations. How does the church currently train clergy to deal with unwanted pregnancy and abortion? In certain seminary classes, they will probably be subjected to pro-choice or pro-life arguments; in either case, they may only accept or agree with the line of reasoning that they already subscribe to. The implicit message our seminarians get is, Follow your political convictions without intruding on the woman's privacy. Because there is no clear theology underpinning all Christian denominations on the issue, most seminary classes revert to either pro-life or pro-choice argumentation. Concepts like community and hospitality never enter the conversation because the discourses of rights and the philosophical analyses of the beginning of life are more highly developed and thus more pervasive. In light of an ethic of care, this training is patently unacceptable.

Second, the church must understand that what two Christians have created, whether wanted or unwanted, belongs not only to them but also to the entire community. If the church is the Body of Christ, what happens to one member happens to all. The congregation(s) must understand that people with unwanted pregnancies are making choices about something that, in a very real sense, belongs to all of them. If the baby is to be born, it will be baptized into their collective world, and will become part of each member's life; if the fetus is to be aborted, it will be represented only by a hole, by a lack of relationship and love in the life of every member. Thus, the church has a stake in the reproductive decisions of all Christians.[11] Although no congregation can demand that one of its members either have an abortion or have a baby, I suggest that she (and the father) owe their congregation(s) a conversation about why they have made the choices they have. Christians must work to ensure that this conversation does not function as an exercise in humiliation or intimidation but rather understand it as vitally necessary so that the church can begin to comprehend the realities associated with unwanted pregnancy. The congregation, then, needs such a conversation in order to correct the ills and oppression these women must bear.

Thus, rather than blaming the woman for her choice of abortion, congregation members need to hold themselves responsible for the things that block this woman from having a child. Furthermore, the congregation should attempt to remove the things that keep this woman or this couple from having their baby. If the woman is afraid that she will be expelled from her high school or Christian college, or will lose her scholarship if the university finds out she is pregnant, the church should picket the school until policy is changed. If the woman is afraid she will lose her job, the parish should exert pressure on the workplace to change its rules, and should strive to provide the woman with an equivalent job. If the woman is afraid to raise the baby, the congregation should step in and offer anything that is needed, including housing, support, even another family to raise the baby. Even if a particular woman decides that she must choose abortion, the congregation should still attempt to make the world a safer place for her to have a baby, because in so doing, the world might be made safer for the next woman with an unwanted pregnancy in that community. Whatever any woman (for any reason) would lose for carrying her baby to term should be redressed and supplied by her church.

Today's congregations can only respond this way, I suggest, if they understand that what is growing inside that woman's body is part of the life of the church. The sacrifices that one could and would make for one's own children should be made for this woman and her child, for if a church is truly functioning as a body of Christ, they will indeed be part of one another. Today's churchpeople, in attempting to respect each other's privacy, have drifted from this commitment to solidarity. And in the individualistic, autonomous church that we so often inhabit, it is single women with unwanted pregnancies who are most often left alone, abandoned.

On the other hand, our churches need to be careful not to use new, community-based orientations toward abortion as a way to persecute Christian women. They must understand that women's need for abortion stems from the fact that when babies are conceived, we are the ones to carry them within our bodies; when babies are born, we are most often the ones who must alter our lives to meet their needs. At different times and in many cases, this situation is unsatisfactory to us. We have come to believe, as a result of cultural shifts of the last thirty years or so, that we ought to have the opportunity to pursue meaningful careers and work outside the home to the same degree as our husbands and brothers. We can become good doctors, lawyers, businesswomen, university professors, and even good ministers, but we cannot do so if we have to carry and care for too many children. Even if we are lucky enough to afford childcare during the day, we still have to come home to what used to be the full-time job of taking care of the house and kids. Whatever the level of difficulty, power, and pay our job has, coming home at night to kids who need our care and attention functions to diminish our capacities to do well at whatever we're trying to do. For many Christian women, abortion may be necessary for survival.

Therefore, I suggest that as Christians focus attention on the communal component of raising children, they must also be careful not to become engaged in any sort of war against pregnant women. The church can only make available everything within its means to let women with unwanted pregnancies know that they and their babies are welcome while they are in the process of making their decisions. Once a woman makes it to an abortion clinic, I believe that any intervention or protest there ceases to be an offering of support and becomes harassment. To attempt to stop abortion at the site of an abortion clinic is to enter the problem much too late. We cannot demand that any woman carry a pregnancy to term, even if it is for the sake of "our" children, for to do so is another form of keeping women in their place and denying them full access to the grace-filled community that God and our churches promise.

Our attention to the developing fetuses must always recognize that every fetus lives inside a woman. Today, many commentators speak of "fetal environments" and "childbearers," language which attempts to erase the fact that a particular woman offers her body for nine months so that another human being can live. Such an action can only be understood as a gift. As Christians, I believe that we should never force a woman to make that choice, either by directly prohibiting abortion or by threatening to exclude her from our church if she chooses abortion. Rather, we must work so that Christian women will want to carry children—whether they can keep them or not—in order to return that child to the arms of an open, loving church. If we force women to carry unwanted children against their desires and better judgments, we are not living in the community we seek; although we might gain children, we do so at the cost of our women.

This model, I suggest, resonates with those presented in both casuistry and an ethics of caring, emphasizing community, relationships, and context. The practice of casuistry in the confessional, we will recall, stood, at least initially for public confession in front of the entire community. Even well into the Middle Ages, decisions about correlative penances were not made in private, but constituted a large public debate dependent on the community of the church. In the work of Carol Gilligan, community functions in a less abstract way. That is, while there is no theorization of particular communities such as "church," each person is understood to be deeply and inextricably embedded in particular communities. Each person is a husband, wife, or companion to someone, a child to someone else, a parent, perhaps, to others. Each person has friends and acquaintances and correlative responsibilities to those relationships. "Knowing what to do," in Gilligan's model, involves understanding and evaluating the intricacies of these relationships. My model for a contemporary church dealing with an unwanted pregnancy, I suggest, reflects both of these community-oriented insights. The pastor, by refusing to help the pregnant woman as an isolated individual, stands in for and eventually leads her to the larger community. The community members state their claim on and their responsibilities toward this woman, and in so doing recognize and honor the role that she and her baby have in their life. The kinds of relationships discussed by Gilligan become a source of support in this church rather than things to hide from.

Both casuistry and caring hold that principles are important to the moral life, and both therefore avoid slipping into any one of the various brands of relativism or emotivism. However, casuistry and caring avoid the counterbalanced legalism associated with rules and maxims by understanding that every case happens in a context. In both models, primary attention is paid to that context in a way that allows us to compensate for the complications of everyday life. The combination of casuistry and caring allows us to see that moral evaluation is not something to be applied to an isolated act, but rather something that can enhance many aspects of the larger context.

Morality is not a legalistic project of evaluating isolated actions, but rather an endeavor to seek a better life for all community members. Thus, while we, in any particular church, may be guided by our beliefs that abortion is either wrong or right, we also acknowledge that morality must be determined case by case. A whole new church could emerge as a result of reminding our pastors that no woman gets pregnant by herself, and by having those pastors remind their congregations that each member of that church looses something with every abortion. Rather than a community that needs protection from the presence of unwanted pregnancy, the church could become a place where women come to find support and a family for themselves and their unborn children.

When I speak to church-sponsored meetings and seminaries about abortion, ministers and seminarians often try to convince me that they already are supporting women with unwanted pregnancies in their churches. When I ask what that support looks like, they tell me that they bring such women bags of groceries or send a small check. These well-meaning Christians often cannot understand why more women in their parishes don't choose adoption rather than abortion. They are fighting hard against abortion, they explain to me. They spend a lot of time in front of clinics and on picket lines. They give money to right-to-life organizations and even go on rescues. They write their congresspeople and attend meetings to support laws which prohibit abortion. What more can they do, they ask. I suggest that as long as Christians see themselves as pro-life or pro-choice (or, for Catholics, a proponent of either double effect or proportionalism), we will be a divided church, at odds with our brothers and sisters. In order to respond more faithfully to the rich moral norms of community and hospitality, we must lay down these divisive ideologies. We must surrender the idea that it is more important to adhere to an abstract principle than it is to care for our neighbors. The fierce oppositions involved in today's abortion wars only serve to divide the church and prevent us from caring about and responding morally to each other. Only when we transcend these absolutist ideologies, can we begin to go about the business of being the church.

CHAPTER SEVEN

Subjectivity, Fragmentation, and the Law
An Argument for Repeal

—◄o►—

> *The question is not how to paste and staple a consensus*
> *together again but rather to live culturally and politically*
> *with fragmentation.*

Catherine Stimpson

The first four chapters of this book recounted the ways that "abortion" is constructed in several competing communities of discourse: liberal, Roman Catholic, evangelical, and feminist. Each of these systems "see" different things in the intervention, each has different ideas about where the world ought to be headed, each has a different method for working toward its particular telos. I argued that there is no one thing that is accurately or adequately called "abortion," and that the differences surrounding their constructions actually render "abortion" a different moral action in each of these worlds.

Each of these discourses "make sense" to me because each of these communities has helped to form me. I feel comfortable enough in each of these four worlds to "see" abortion the way its members see it. I find a vantage point for one world by standing, temporarily, in another; I can then move back to the first and look at the second. The places where moral convictions simply do not translate, and the shifts and changes in a particular discourse, reflect the locations of my own confusions. Part of my fieldwork, then, has taken place inside myself, disrupting the traditional distinction between emic and etic, between being outside a culture and part of one. This chapter examines how the oscillation between these competing autobiographies works for and inside my life. In this way, I hope to draw some conclusions about how competing communities exist inside many of us, conclusions which I believe have implications for American law.

Like many people, I am a member of more than one community at any given time. My ability to see the world (and the issue of abortion) one way at one time and another way later is produced by the logics of the systems which make the world intelligible to me, namely, the feminism to which I now adhere, the Christian principles that continue to offer me hope, the Catholicism of my youth, and the American liberalism that surrounds us all. Thus, although I am a feminist, I find myself wondering sometimes if the Christian goal of welcoming all children—even those that are unwanted by those who conceive them—isn't a good way to live. Conversely, although I try to be faithful to my Christian heritage, I am quite frankly baffled by the church's lack of interest in women's lives. And both of these refrains intersect with the precept of technological progress; sometimes I think technology can be used to advance those ideologies I believe are good, while at other times it seems only harmful and destructive. Sometimes when I look at the issue of abortion I see only women, other times only abandoned babies (like myself). Sometimes when I look at my own conflicted feelings, I believe that the debate is unsolvable.

Internal conflicts like these can also be seen in the growing literature produced by women who have had abortions. For example, a woman named Christina, described in Sue Hertz's *Caught in the Crossfire,* was sixteen, pregnant from the first time she had made love with her high-school sweetheart, and scared. A lovely girl with long curly black hair and round blue eyes fringed with dark lashes, she walked toward the clinic steps, her father and boyfriend trailing behind her, [both supporting the impending abortion]. "You don't want to do this," an old man shouted, "you're killing your baby." Raised Roman Catholic, Christina was already unsure of her decision to abort. She froze in place on the sidewalk, sobbing.[1]

Such confusions arise, I believe, because competing frameworks hold us. We believe one thing, and at the same time we believe something completely contradictory. Our convictions are splintered, our loyalties divided. Our ambivalence signifies the fact that we live in complicated worlds. "I was very torn," a pro-choice woman named Darla writes in Rita Townsend and Ann Perkins's *Bitter Fruit*. "I went in [to the abortion clinic] thinking that I was going to [have an abortion], but when I saw it on the ultrasound, I couldn't do it."[2] At the moment that Darla saw the ultrasound, two worlds were competing within her to define the meaning of "it." One world told her that what was inside her was no more than a group of cells, a "product of conception." She should have "it" removed and get on with her life. Another implored her to see on that screen a baby, a human life. Many women who make difficult decisions between abortion and unwanted pregnancy experience a similar conflict. Unwanted pregnancy often alters perceptions and beliefs. Their new "situation" is not adequately addressed by their old convictions. They feel confusion, fragmentation, and pain.

This kind of pain and loss prompts philosophers to promulgate theories of wholeness, unity, and coherent subjectivity for human life. These theories comfort us by explaining that we are whole beings, that our choice in difficult circumstances will be clear, that we owe allegiance only to one ideology. In the theory of liberal unified subjectivity, there is no room for a competing or contentious voice. We are, they say, whole, one, unbroken. But as any woman who has faced an unwanted pregnancy knows, wholeness is a trait few of us are able to sustain. The coherence and continuity of an "individual" are not necessary, logical, or natural features, but products of a way we have been taught to think about personhood, about what a "person" ought to be. "Coherence," in the words of Mary Poovey, "is a property that belongs to our ideas about [personhood] and to many of the institutionalizations of those ideas, not a property of the human subject."[3] Theories that suggest we are coherent beings obscure the deep ideological conflicts in our lives. Conflicts over abortion remind us that people are often fragmented, not fully contained by one discourse. Participation in any one community or discourse, for many of us, is never complete. There is always something else in us that must find sustenance elsewhere. While "we" are still the same biological matter from one context to another, everything else can change.[4]

Yet the concept and assertion of the unified individual is omnipresent in American society. We have become so convinced that we are internally coherent subjects that we are not able to see the multiple discourses fighting through us. We believe that our pleasure and happiness reside in our ability to know ourselves as a participant in only one system. We are convinced that sanity rests in our capacity to predict permanently how we will see and interpret the world. When internal conflicts do arise, we say "I changed my mind" or, more often, ignore them. Our desperate belief that we are whole, boundaried selves shapes the way we experience and ignore competing internal discourses, and forms the theoretical basis for many social conflicts today, including most prominently the abortion debate.

Although our investment in this unified subjectivity makes it difficult for most of us to conceptualize the human fetus outside that frame, several theorists have done so. Iris Marion Young, for example, describes her own pregnancy as follows:

> Reflection on the experience of pregnancy reveals a body subjectivity that is decentered, myself in the mode of not being myself. As my pregnancy begins, I experience it as a change in my body; I become different from what I have been. My nipples become reddened and tender; my belly swells into a pear. I feel elastic around my waist, itching, this round, hard middle replacing the doughy belly with which I still identify. Then I feel a little tickle, a little gurgle in my belly. It is my feeling, my insides, and it feels somewhat like a gas bubble, but it is not; it is different, in another place, belonging to another, another that is nevertheless my body. The first movements of the fetus produce this sense of the splitting subject; the fetus's movements are wholly mine, completely within me, conditioning my experiences and space. Only I have access to these movements, for months only I can witness this life within me, and it is only under my direction of where to put their hands that others can feel these movements. . . . Pregnancy challenges the integration of my body experience by rendering fluid the boundary between what is within, myself, and what is outside, separate. I experience my insides as the space of another, yet my own body.[5]

In a like manner, Catherine MacKinnon describes the fetus growing inside a woman's body as

> more than a body part but less than a person, where it is, is largely what it is. From the standpoint of the pregnant woman, it is both me and not me. It "is" the pregnant woman in the sense that it is in her and it is hers more than anyone's. It "is not" her in the sense that she is all there is. In a legal system that views the individual as a unitary self, and that self as a bundle of rights, it is no wonder that the pregnant woman has eluded legal grasp, and her fetus with her.[6]

What most of us see when we imagine a fetus, however, is either a full, moral subject (an unborn child) or a mere collection of cells.

Thomas Amy   3/13

Chorus

HQ
767.5
U5
C48

2

Carp and assume the fish tastes bad. This is not a particu
taste. Second, they do tend to be bony, and have some b
extra effort, these can be dealt with easily enough. The b
them.

If you are still interested in eating Asian Carp, check out
Missouri):
Flying Fish, Great Dish (Part 1: Introduction & Removir
http://www.youtube.com/watch?v=T1NVUV8yhmU

Flying Fish, Great Dish (Part 2: Making "Flying Carp W
http://www.youtube.com/watch?v=CB-fmA07gZ8

Flying Fish, Great Dish (Part 3: Deboning Filets & Closi
http://www.youtube.com/watch?v=RhGkjwxm_0o

**As is often reported, did Asian Carp first escape into
floods?** NO. In some respects, the truth is actually scarie
in the early 1970s. It did not take long before they escap
was in 1974 or 1975. The first Bighead Carp was caught
them into the wild. They are quite adept at escaping on t

As is often reported, do Asian Carp make up 90% of
There are certainly a lot of Asian Carp in these rivers. No
were 40 years ago, when there were no Asian Carp. But
many there are today. For example, see the following qu
"These quotes on biomass in the Mississippi River or Illi

We have a hard time conceptualizing the fetus as both part and not part of its mother because liberal ideology has trained our eyes to register only whole, boundaried human subjects. Human subjectivity is either present or absent in our philosophy; there is no room for an ontological in-between. There is no way to comprehend a fetus as both part of the mother and a separate being, or a woman as being more than one subject (but less than two) during pregnancy. She is either a woman (who happens to be pregnant) or a pregnant woman (the bearer of another separate human being).[7] The differences between these two views is at the heart of the abortion debate.

Because our eyes are trained to see the world (and all pregnancies in it) only in terms of fully present human subjects, some of us see the pregnant woman as the only subject involved in a pregnancy. She is a person with concrete and tangible edges and a full composite of social rights. From this view, the fetus is not a human subject worthy of attention, and abortion is completely acceptable because only one person (the woman) is ever involved. Other people, however, see the fetus inside her as a full person, equal in importance to the mother from the moment of its conception. The fact that this fetus resides in and requires a woman's body for its own existence is of little consequence in this worldview. Here, there are two subjects, both of which command the rights that accompany human subjectivity in the liberal system. And because both subjects have rights, a fetus's right to live is more important than any reason a woman might have for killing it.

The abortion wars are waged, then, primarily because the law can only conceptualize unified subjects: either a fetus is a full subject and has the right not to be "killed" or it is not, and a woman has a right to control her reproductive capacities. "Woman's rights" are pitted against the "rights of the unborn" because—within the liberal system of American law—we have no other way of conceiving human beings than as fully coherent individuals who need protection from one another. The abortion conflict cannot be resolved, then, until we have more ways of seeing the human fetus than these two, and more ways of understanding competing moralities than pro-life and pro-choice.

Several recent proposals attempt to transcend the current polarization. Ronald Dworkin, for example, recognizes that the abortion conflict will not be resolved until we rethink the moral status of the fetus because "the question of whether a fetus is a human being, either at conception or at some later point in pregnancy, is simply too ambiguous to be useful."[8] In his *Life's Dominion,* he proposes a third alternative, that the human fetus has an intrinsic, innate value from conception, although it does not acquire the interests or rights of the liberal subject until birth. Abortion is wrong, according to Dworkin, not because it murders another fully righted human being, but rather "because it disregards and insults the intrinsic value, the sacred character, of any stage or form of human life."[9]

Dworkin asserts that most of us already believe that abortion is something in between murder and birth control and therefore, according to him, we already recognize that a fetus has value.[10] He construes this value as "sacredness," although he is very clear that this sacredness need not necessarily take on religious connotations, closer possibly, "to Walt Whitman's 'procreant urge of the world,' or David Plante's 'elemental pulse of the mind.'"[11] Thus, according to Dworkin, we intrinsically recognize that abortion is more wrong in some cases than in others, more wrong when a fetus is destroyed for purposes of convenience than when a greater good (such as the life or general well-being of the woman) follows from the abortion. In a like manner, Dworkin argues that we all intrinsically recognize that the destruction of healthy fetuses is a bigger tragedy than the destruction of defective fetuses.[12] By appealing to what he believes are general moral sensibilities, Dworkin offers a reconception of the fetus that he believes will function as a compromise for the two opposing sides of the abortion war.

Similarly, according to Elizabeth Mensch and Alan Freeman's *The Politics of Virtue,* the status of the fetus should be discussed not in relation to the question of personhood, but rather within a frame that accommodates questions about the meaning and value of life. Mensch and Freeman argue that the fetus is a potential human being, and that we can only rightly understand abortion when we contemplate the meaning of death. According to them, America has lost its ability to discuss the meaning of life and death because we have become polarized along secular and religious lines. Before the 1960s, they argue, the major ethical debates took place between Roman Catholic natural law methodology and neo-orthodox Protestant methodology. Although these traditions of moral reasoning differed, they shared enough presumptions about the value of life and the meaning of death that conversation was possible. Today, because secular America can no longer talk about death, conversations about abortion are unintelligible.

Mensch and Freeman suggest that although we believe that we keep religion separate from public life, religious thought and religious traditions have affected our value systems and cannot be easily separated from public discourse. Religion and politics thus operate in a dialectic, reinforcing each other. Where political and legal structures ensure order in daily life, religion addresses the issue of our own mortality and lends meaning to our finitude. Religion helps us "to confront our obligation toward life regarded as a gift from God."[13] Therefore, Mensch and Freeman suggest, our public debates regarding abortion would be more intelligible and productive if we would acknowledge the religious underpinnings of American culture and the religious component of this dialectic. Such a turn to religion "does not require biblical literalism or political conservatism," but will help us discuss abortion in terms of life and death without assuming the inherent rightness or wrongness of abortion. That is, while abortion is neither right nor wrong, remembering that life is a gift from God will help us reach a compromise in the middle, a solution "which allows abortion while regulating it to some degree and also seek[s] ways to discourage it."[14]

Dworkin, Mensch, and Freeman theorize the human fetus as something outside the frame of the existing dichotomy, as something other than either a human being with full rights or nothing. They argue that most Americans already see or could see a middle ground in which the fetus is neither fully human nor a nonexistent entity, in which abortion, therefore, is neither fully right nor fully wrong. They do so in the hope that this argument will constitute an acceptable compromise to both pro-choice and pro-life ideology: pro-choice advocates will accept the compromise because the fetus will be treated as less than a fully righted subject, and pro-life adherents will accept it because the fetus will be treated as more than nothing. These middle-ground proposals are designed to absorb conflicting constructions by offering mediating solutions. They assume that consensus can be reached on the value of fetal (and human) life through a discussion that acknowledges the sacredness or meaning of life.

In their attempt at a more complex understanding of the fetus, Dworkin, Mensch, and Freeman assume that all interpreters will or can transcend their particular communities to agree on the value of fetal life. That is, in each proposal, everyone who encounters this fetus that is "in-between" ought to come to the same conclusion: fetal life is sacred though not fully human; the destruction of a fetus is bad, and so on. However, I suggest that while these propositions will seem intelligible to some, they will not be persuasive to many others.

For many people, the meaning and value of the fetus cannot be altered by fiat. It is impossible for me to imagine, for example, that any of these compromises would appeal to all four of the communities we've reviewed. What would prompt those evangelicals who believe that abortion is always wrong to agree that fetuses are not full human beings with rights to life? Similarly, what would impel a feminist who sees no difference between birth control and abortion to see the group of cells inside her as "sacred"? What would induce traditional Catholics to surrender natural law teaching, or evangelicals to forgo the authority of Scripture, or feminists to abandon their woman-centered analysis in favor of a methodology based on contemplation about "the meaning of death" or "the sacredness of life"?

Indeed, the compromise proposals of Dworkin, Freeman, and Mensch are set on terms that protect what the authors themselves believe to be the fundamental principles of justice and human life. Mensch and Freeman advocate the use of religion in the abortion debate because religion addresses their questions about the meaning of life and death. To someone who does not have such questions, or to one who formulates them differently, Mensch and Freeman's descriptions of the fetus (as life) and of abortion (as death) might be unrecognizable. Similarly, Dworkin theorizes that life is sacred from conception, but to someone whose eyes see those few, dependent cells as an encroachment on their freedom, Dworkin's description makes no sense.[15] These compromises will not be persuasive to most participants in the current debate precisely because the value of fetal life is constructed, as I have shown, community by community.

Other works propose a compromise of a different sort: rather than discussing abortion in the frame of sacred value and the meaning of life, these texts hold up tolerance as the ideal that will release us from the abortion conflict. According to Roger Rosenblatt's *Life Itself*, for example, although abortion is a bad thing and ought to be discouraged, it must be permitted in American culture today because we are a nation that believes in personal freedom. We must accept the fact, Rosenblatt claims, that some women—for their own private reasons—find abortion necessary. He argues that all Americans should recognize as part of their commitment to American pluralism that the private beliefs of others should be respected. Consequently, our attitude toward abortion should be "permissive but discouraging."[16] This permissive attitude is correlated with the ideals of the liberal state, where different opinions on abortion are acceptable only as long as those differences do not interfere with our overriding commitment to tolerance. That is, while an individual may hold contradictory or conflicted views in private, in public space he or she must appear rational, coherent, self-contained, and tolerant.[17]

Compromises such as Rosenblatt's assume that every individual in America is committed to overcoming, or at least overlooking, cross-traditional differences. That is, he assumes that an individual's commitment to the political philosophy of American liberalism takes precedent over any other, particularistic conviction. In my research, I did not find this to be true for most communities involved in the abortion debate. Moreover, the appeal to pluralism asks us to overlook our own internal conflicts over abortion. That is, we must give priority to the part of subjectivity that identifies itself as an American citizen; everything else can only exist in private spaces. To my thinking, the pluralist option isn't itself a solution to the problem of competing discourses but simply a reassertion of one of those discourses. The very idea that it is good to tolerate difference is part of one construction: liberal ideology. For those who participate in communities that do not underwrite pluralist presuppositions, tolerance may in fact be discouraged.[18]

Moreover, I suggest that when people express middle-of-the-road opinions such as Rosenblatt's "permissive but discouraging" attitude, it is most often not because they are unified subjects who believe that such an inconsistent position is desirable. Indeed, like the women I described above who simultaneously believe mutually exclusive assertions about abortion, most people who stand in the middle of the road do so as a way of negotiating their own competing constructions of abortion. It is not the case that conflicting beliefs and ideas exist comfortably within the frame of mediated positions such as Rosenblatt's. Rather, in internal compromises, competing constructions exist in a tense, suppressed stand-off. Moreover, such compromises only reify the importance of liberal individualism. I will suggest below that a better solution exists in investigating the competing structures within the individual.

In a work which resembles that of Mensch and Freeman, Ruth Colker proposes a somewhat different solution to the abortion problem, in which contemporary feminist theology and spirituality can influence abortion legislation. In her view, feminist theology instructs us to approach moral quandaries such as abortion with attention to and appreciation for the principles of love, compassion, and wisdom, which will lead us to "live in a community of connected selves." The right to privacy (upon which current abortion laws are based) does not reflect the connected society she envisions; the right to equality, by contrast, "does not rely on assumptions about lack of connectedness." In her thinking, "equality doctrine, at its core, requires that people be treated with equal respect" and therefore serves as a better foundation for abortion in a connected world.[19] While I am sympathetic to any project which advocates relatedness, it is unclear to me how Colker achieves connectedness on the grounds of equality without falling back into the liberal, individuated subject. As I argued in chapter 5, equality offers insufficient conceptual grounds for adequate abortion politics, as it very often means that women and children are left unprotected because the state denies any obligation to childcare or childrearing. The idea of equality is inadequate because its traditional norm—the subject that everyone is equal to—is the unencumbered (non–child bearing) male. Equality means, as I have argued, the freedom to be like men; moreover, it focuses attention on "women's (reproductive) difference" and reinforces the stereotypes that lead to sexism.

Peter Wenz offers yet another argument for abortion rights, based not on tolerance, privacy, or equality, but rather on religious freedom. He suggests that the ground of privacy articulated in *Roe v. Wade* be replaced by the ideal of religious freedom because "religious freedom accords best with the words of the Constitution and with Supreme Court decisions in a variety of areas."[20] This is true, he believes, because "arguments about the personhood and right to life of young fetuses are structurally and epistemologically identical to arguments about the existence of God."[21] I suggest, however, that the argument of religious freedom is deficient precisely because it is still the government that "grants" that freedom along with the right to abort. Because the state is the granting institution, it alone has ultimate power to define which parts of our identities are allowed to appear in public, and which parts—such as religion—remain sequestered. By making abortion a legal issue on any grounds, we give priority to the unified, public individual and solidify our commitment to liberal thinking. American law cannot adjudicate the needs, conditions, or concerns of other communities because it places itself and the legal, unified subject above the debate.

In lieu of these proposals of consensus, compromise, or tolerance, I offer the following solution. Because, as I have demonstrated, morality is constructed by competing ideological discourses, it ought to be the task of each tradition to regulate abortion, reproduction, and sexuality inside its own boundaries. Rather than expending time and money to alter and influence legislation, I believe that each tradition should spend more time and money instead on making its world more plausible, internally coherent, and attractive. For example, if as I argued in chapter 6, Christians see the world as a place where children ought to be welcomed, believers should work to make adoption services more humane and available; they should strive to make single mothers with unwanted pregnancies feel accepted and honored; they should live and act in ways that would allow pregnant women to feel positively about surrendering their babies to a Christian community. In so doing, Christians would allow people to participate in their entire community-based worldview, rather than forcing their opinions on others with different ideologies. In the same vein, if, as I argued in chapter 5, feminists see the world as a place where women ought to be able to exercise self-definition in both sexuality and reproduction, they ought to work to make birth control, abortion, and economic resources more available. Feminists ought to be striving against the things that make childrearing the exclusive burden of women and working toward ways in which raising children receives the support of the wider community. I suggest that the battle over abortion ought not take place in the courts or legislatures but within the interpretive realms of particular communities. Competing ideologies should be fighting to make their worldviews intelligible and attractive to others, not fighting in the courtrooms over the legal status of abortion. As I argued in the last two chapters, the narrowness of the contemporary abortion debate ideologically blocks communities from exhibiting and working toward their perception of the common good. It behooves all competing ideologies to focus their energy and attention on advancing their entire worldviews rather than on lobbying for pro-choice or pro-life legislation.

This will best be accomplished, I suggest, by the repeal of all abortion laws. By repeal, I mean that Americans should stop viewing abortion as a legal issue that should be settled for all people and begin to see "abortion" as a collection of activities whose moralities are pegged to community norms. Repeal does not mean that a given community will simply be tolerant of differences in other groups; rather, it recognizes that the ethical evaluation is dependent on the worldview of the participants and cannot be determined beforehand for all people. It will be helpful here to reiterate Ninia Baehr's description of repeal, quoted in chapter 4:

> If you repeal something from the law, you take it out of the law entirely. If you legalize something, you grant control to the state. For example, alcohol is legal in this country, but the government doesn't trust each person to regulate her own relationship with alcohol. It tells her how old she must be to drink it, when and where she may buy it—and it changes the laws about alcohol as it sees fit. This is not true, say, of orange juice. The criminal code does not mention orange juice. The government lets us drink it when, where and how we want to. The FDA still checks to make sure that the orange juice is safe. The government will even help us pay for our orange juice if we receive food stamps. Other than playing this supportive role, the government is silent on the matter of orange juice.[22]

I suggest that the government should likewise be silent on the matter of abortion precisely because it cannot take into account the realities of each communal context and therefore cannot pass judgment on the morality of the intervention.

With repeal, each tradition could concentrate its resources on accomplishing the goal of displaying its goods to others. In devoting all our attention to *Roe* we do not really achieve compromise, but a sullen, fragile standoff. By not privileging the legal, liberal subject, churches and feminist communities can release themselves from the system which grants hegemony to the unified, coherent, public subject. They can spend more time, energy, and money working toward understandings and institutions that challenge the assumption that we are independent, isolated, detached beings.

In advocating repeal, I do not mean to promote a social order in which anyone can do anything they want in private (as long as it does not conflict with the commitment to be tolerant in public). My point is not that "abortion means different things to different people, and therefore everyone should do what she or he wants," for such a formulation is a restatement of the liberal, pluralist agenda. Instead, I suggest that communities change and influence the opinions of others not through legislation but through persuading opponents that theirs is the better way of life. This can not be accomplished either by influencing legislation or by offering thin compromises regarding the value of human life; it can only be achieved as each community demonstrates its entire way of life—and especially the goods offered in that life—to outsiders. Removing abortion from the realm of legal discourse frees every community to display their lives and worlds in ways that will attract new participants. A tradition only "wins" in the abortion debate when a woman with an unwanted pregnancy sees the hope and possibilities offered to her by that tradition and changes her interpretation of her pregnancy as a result. Thus, I suggest not only that abortion laws be repealed, but that each community commit itself to practicing its beliefs in such a way that new people will be attracted. Although repeal doesn't guarantee that every community will move in this positive direction, I do believe that once the conflict is taken out of the legal realm, members will have more funds and energy to revitalize the entire moral fabric of their communities.

In my view, repeal of abortion laws will not end the abortion wars; rather, it will give them a critically different inflection. That is, we will no longer be fighting about whether the procedure should or shouldn't be legal; we will be fighting about the fundamental differences between worldviews and communities. We will no longer be concerned with arguing over a particular point of law: rather, we will participate in larger projects which display, for example, how and why feminism is a necessary political orientation for all human beings or how the vision of God's grace leads us to the new creation and why we find that desirable. In a sense, then, repeal raises the abortion debate to a more meaningful level, a level which asks us to explain not only what we believe but why. Speaking as a feminist and a Christian, this is a debate worth having.

The repeal of abortion laws would speak to the concerns of many forms of feminism. Rather than arguing for legal abortion on the grounds of rights or privacy, we could devote ourselves to helping other women obtain the things they need to exercise their reproductive freedom. Moreover, repeal of abortion laws would allow us to move beyond the arguments for legalized abortion into social orders where we can live out our convictions about the value of women in culture. We could expend our energies experimenting with the kinds of worlds we dream about.

Christians of all sorts could benefit from repeal as well.[23] In today's logic, denominational leaders are forced into taking a stand on *Roe v. Wade,* into answering the question "Should abortion be legal?" By recognizing this as the wrong question, churches and denominational bodies would be able to recognize that the most appropriate Christian method for dealing with abortion will be to provide more effective assistance to women with unwanted pregnancies. In transcending the pro-life/pro-choice debate, every Christian congregation would be free to respond with programs designed to remove the things that prevent women with unwanted pregnancies from having babies. For any Christian denomination or organization to pour huge amounts of time or energy in an attempt to control the legal climate is immoral. In so doing, Christian organizations are inadvertently promoting a theory of individualism which ultimately serves to confine religion to the private sphere and to render religious tenets secondary to the primacy of citizenship. Not until repeal— not until we are free from the need to fight the legal battle—will Christians, for example, be able to provide the services that they ought to provide as the Body of Christ.[24]

Repeal would also lessen the tendency of individuals to think about their attitudes toward abortion as either pro-life or pro-choice. In the logic of today's debate, no other alternatives exist. The binary that currently exists separates pro-life from pro-choice in a way that preempts and obstructs conversations. In reducing our differences into two ideologies, the details that give communities both political substance and moral character are lost. With repeal, the dichotomous stronghold of pro-choice and pro-life will cease to exist; we will no longer be required to be unified selves who place our allegiance on one side or the other. Without such a concrete divide, we will be able to think of ourselves as owing allegiance to more than one tradition. We will no longer need to believe that we are whole, coherent, or unified; we can attend to those internal voices that register dissent without worrying that our "position on abortion" will be compromised, challenged, or shattered. Through repeal, we would be able to emphasize, as Poovey states, "not the ways in which subjects are isolatable, autonomous, centered individuals, but the ways in which each person has conflicting interests and complex ties to other, apparently autonomous individuals with similar (and different) interests and needs."[25] In breaking open the dichotomy of pro-life and pro-choice, we can attend to the nonunitary ways that many of us already live.

At the same time, these nonunitary practices will allow us to see our essential connections to others; finally we can locate ourselves within communities with recognizable, historical ideologies. That is, we can recognize that our selves do not simply consist of random, detached fragments but rather are made up of scraps and segments that are affected by and conjoined with other selves. When the unified, legal subject is banished through repeal, connective practices which already exist—such as feminism's emphasis on collectivity or the church's stress on its obligations as the Body of Christ—can be seen more clearly as transcending the isolating individualism of today's America. Repeal would allow us to bring those visions into the realm of reproduction and childcare; it would help us to live in the world where care and relationship are ethical ideals practiced by everyone. Repeal would help us see not only that we are not unified subjects, but also that we are connected in profound ways to others.

In short, I suggest that repeal would allow us to see the most positive aspects of every community to which we belong precisely because those communities would be spending time, money, and energy to win converts rather than to influence legislation. Our commitment to the better world that feminism brings will be unmediated by the rights language which requires us to be whole, autonomous, and unitary. Moreover, with repeal, we will be able to meditate on the contributions that various religions might have made to our lives without underwriting a system in which our religious affiliations and relationships are sequestered in private space. Through repeal, we can witness more easily our connections with and to each other. When understood within this frame of connectedness and fragmentation, the morality of abortion may shift from something we fight over, from something which divides us into one of two categories, to become an opportunity for us to discover the multiple realities in which we live. Only when abortion ceases to be a legal issue, only when we are no longer compelled to take sides on *Roe v. Wade* as the sole expression of our convictions about abortion, will we be able to examine and map the many moral discourses of abortion. Only then can we show each other what we want our worlds to look like, and how we want our children to fit into them. Only then will we truly be capable of understanding—in any meaningful sense—the ethics of abortion.

Notes

◄○►

INTRODUCTION

1. G. E. M. Anscombe, *Intention* (Ithaca: Cornell University Press, 1962), 37.
2. Ludwig Wittgenstein, *Philosophical Investigations* (1958; New York: Macmillan, 1968), 200.
3. The term ideology has been used in a variety of ways. One of the most common is its use in Marxist discourse to signify a set of ideas that help mystify the real conditions of oppression. However, to my thinking, there is not one "real" reality which ideology obfuscates but rather many competing realities, all constructed by ideological frames. The project of the first half of this book is simply to investigate the competing ideologies surrounding the intervention referred to as abortion.
4. Wittgenstein, *Philosophical Investigations,* 132.

CHAPTER ONE
THE REPRODUCTION OF AMERICA

1. Rayna Rapp in *The Choices We Made,* ed. Angela Bonavoglia (New York: Random House, 1991), 159.
2. Many social histories of the family argue that the configuration of an extended family life was functional not only for rearing disabled children, but for the optimum functioning of rural and agriculturally based

existence as well. See especially Carl Degler, *At Odds: Women and the Family in America from the Revolution to the Present* (Oxford: Oxford University Press, 1980). For social histories of family life, see Lawrence Stone, *The Family, Sex, and Marriage in England, 1500–1800* (New York: Harper, 1977); Philippe Aries, *Centuries of Childhood: A Social History of Family Life* (New York: Vintage, 1962); and Stephanie Coontz, *The Social Origins of Private Life* (London: Verso, 1988).

3. See, for example, Amadeo F. D'Adamo, "Reproductive Technologies: The Two Sides of the Glass Jar," in *Embryos, Ethics, and Women's Rights,* ed. Elaine Hoffman Baruch, Amadeo F. D'Adamo, and Joni Seager (New York: Harrington Park Press, 1988), 25. Regarding the history of the use of amniocentesis in the United States, see Ruth Cowan, "Genetic Autonomy and Reproductive Choice: An Ethics for Autonomy," in *The Code of Codes: Scientific and Social Issues in the Human Genome Project,* ed. Daniel Kevles and Leroy Hood (Cambridge: Harvard University Press, 1992), 244–63.

4. William Ray Arney, *Power and the Profession of Obstetrics* (Chicago: University of Chicago Press, 1982).

5. John Rawls, *A Theory of Justice* (Cambridge: Harvard University Press, 1971), 12.

6. John Rawls, "Kantian Constructivism in Moral Theory," *Journal of Philosophy* 77, no. 9 (September 1980): 518–19.

7. Ibid., 518; John Rawls, "Justice as Fairness: Political Not Metaphysical," *Philosophy and Public Affairs* 14, no. 3 (summer 1985): 225.

8. For an argument that Rawls's formulation is both metaphysical and ontological, see Michael Sandel, *Liberalism and the Limits of Justice* (New York: Cambridge University Press, 1982). Sandel's task in this book is to render Rawls's formulation internally inconsistent.

9. Rawls, *A Theory of Justice,* 465.

10. As doctors and researchers face a world where many types of medical resources are scarce, they are forced to make difficult decisions about what kinds of people should receive life-sustaining attention. When problems (such as test results which indicate abnormality) arise, the decisions that are made are often implicitly grounded in a valorized rationality. Similarly, it is not the case that development of new technologies

is consciously grounded in the quest for rationality. Rather, the material conditions of funding and publication within which researchers do their work mask the complexities of social process and the indirectness with which ideology and ideological assumptions operate. In short, it never occurs to the doctors and researchers to make other choices.

11. D'Adamo, "Reproductive Technologies," 16.

12. Rayna Rapp, "Moral Pioneers: Women, Men, and Fetuses on a Frontier of Reproductive Technology," in Hoffman et al., *Embryos, Ethics and Women's Rights,* 110.

13. Daniel Callahan, *What Kind of Life: The Limits of Medical Progress* (New York: Simon and Schuster, 1990), 53.

14. Barbara Katz Rothman, *The Tentative Pregnancy: Prenatal Diagnosis and the Future of Motherhood* (New York: Penguin, 1987), 5.

15. For example, see Rapp, "Moral Pioneers," 101, 110. Rapp claims that the abortion rate after defect is detected is 100 percent.

16. Rothman, *The Tentative Pregnancy,* 4.

17. Barbara Katz Rothman, "Reproductive Technology and the Commodification of Life," in Hoffman et al., *Embryos, Ethics, and Women's Rights,* 97.

18. Cowan, "Genetic Autonomy," 246.

19. Arney, *Power and the Profession of Obstetrics,* 183, emphasis added.

20. Ruth Hubbard, "Eugenics: New Tools, Old Ideas," in Hoffman et al., *Embryos, Ethics, and Women's Rights,* 232.

21. See, for example, Daniel Kevles, *In the Name of Eugenics: Genetics and the Uses of Human Heredity* (Berkeley: University of California Press, 1985), 100.

22. See, for example, Anne Finger, "Claiming All of Our Bodies: Reproductive Rights and Disability," in *Test-Tube Women: What Future for Motherhood,* ed. Rita Arditti, Renate Klein, and Shelley Minden (London: Pandora Press, 1984), 288.

23. Susan Wendell, "Toward a Feminist Theory of Disability," *Hypatia* 4, no. 2 (summer 1989): 104.

24. For example, see E. Virginia Sheppard Lapham's "Living with an Impaired Neonate and Child: A Feminist Issue," in *The Custom-Made Child: Women-Centered Perspectives,* ed. Helen Holmes, Betty Hoskins,

and Michael Gross (Clifton, N.J.: Humana Press, 1981).

25. Allison Davis, "Women with Disabilities: Abortion and Liberation," in *Disability, Handicap, and Society* 2, no. 3 (1987): 275.

26. Michelle Fine and Adrienne Asch, "Shared Dreams: A Left Perspective on Disability Rights and Reproductive Rights," in *Women with Disabilities: Essays in Psychology, Culture, and Politics*, ed. Michelle Fine and Adrienne Asch (Philadelphia: Temple University Press, 1988), 302.

27. Hubbard, "Eugenics," 229.

28. See, for example, Arney, *Power and the Profession of Obstetrics*, 186; and Hubbard, "Eugenics," 227.

29. See, for example, H. Tristram Engelhardt, "Bioethics in Pluralist Societies," *Perspectives in Biology and Medicine* 26, no. 1 (autumn 1982).

30. H. Tristram Engelhardt, *Bioethics and Secular Humanism: The Search for a Common Morality* (London: SCM Press, 1991), 135. Interestingly enough, the fictional character "Dr. Larch" from John Irving's *The Cider House Rules* is an excellent representation of such ideology. Dr. Larch has been performing illegal abortions for many decades and hopes to persuade his best student, against the student's moral convictions, to take up Dr. Larch's practice. "If abortions were legal," exhorts Dr. Larch, "you could refuse—in fact, given your beliefs, you should refuse. But as long as they're against the law, how can you refuse? How can you allow yourself a choice in the matter when there are many women who haven't the freedom to make the choice themselves? The women have no choice. I know you know that's not right, but how can you—you of all people, knowing what you know—HOW CAN YOU FEEL FREE TO CHOOSE NOT TO HELP PEOPLE WHO ARE NOT FREE TO GET OTHER HELP?" (John Irving, *The Cider House Rules* [New York: Bantam Books, 1985], 518, emphasis in original). For Dr. Larch, the personal belief or conviction that abortion is wrong should not obstruct his neighbor's freedom to procure an abortion, even though it means that a doctor must perform those abortions against his own belief system. This is precisely the kind of loyalty that Engelhardt, and the liberal tradition to which he belongs, requires from each of us.

31. Richard Rorty, *Contingency, Irony, Solidarity* (New York: Cambridge University Press, 1989), 189.

32. Ibid.
33. Ibid., 84.
34. H. Tristram Engelhardt, *The Foundations of Bioethics* (New York: Oxford University Press, 1986), 202, 109, 115.
35. Ibid., 118.
36. Ibid., 242.
37. Rothman, *The Tentative Pregnancy*, 186.
38. Ibid., 114.

CHAPTER TWO
THE CATHOLIC CONSTRUCTION OF ABORTION

1. For an excellent resource covering Catholic, Protestant, and secular perspectives, see Merry Bloch Jones, *Birthmothers: Women Who Have Relinquished Babies for Adoption Tell Their Stories* (Chicago: Chicago Review Press, 1993).
2. Joseph Mangan, "An Historical Analysis of the Principle of Double Effect," *Theological Studies* 10 (March 1949): 43.
3. Josef Ghoos, "L'Acte à Double Effet Etude de Theologie Positive," *Ephemerides Theological Loraniese* 27 (1951): 32: "Il est peut-être possible de trouver ailleurs chez saint Thomas des premisses, qui permettent de deduire les principes de l'acte double effet; mais lui-même ne semble pas avoir formellement élaboré ou proposé la doctrine." For further refutation of the assertion that Aquinas introduced the doctrine of double effect, see G. E. M. Anscombe, "Action, Intention, and 'Double Effect,'" in *The Role and Responsibility of the Moral Philosopher*, ed. Daniel Dahlstrom, Desmond Fitzgerald, and John Noonan, Jr. (Washington, D.C.: American Catholic Philosophical Association Press, 1982), 24–25.
4. Double effect is crystallized into these two cases by many theorists. See, for example, Daniel Callahan, *Abortion: Law, Choice, and Morality* (London: Macmillan, 1970), 423; Josef Fuchs, "The Absoluteness of Moral Terms," in *Readings in Moral Theology, no. 1, Moral Norms and Catholic Tradition*, ed. Charles Curran and Richard McCormick (New York: Paulist Press, 1979), 122; Susan Nicholson, *Abortion and the Roman*

Catholic Church (Knoxville, Tenn.: Holston Publishing Company, 1978), 22–36. Nicholson also notes that ectopic pregnancy became licit within double effect thinking only as a result of early-twentieth-century scientific developments which concluded that "from the early stages of pregnancy the tube itself is weakened and dangerous" (30). Prior to this finding, it was believed that the fallopian tube was not pathological until it actually ruptured, and thus abortion in the case of ectopic pregnancy was illicit. Moreover, in Catholic thinking, the fallopian tube must also be removed—even if, medically speaking, it is possible to leave it intact—for the abortion to be considered licit.

5. Ann Taves, *The Household of Faith* (Notre Dame, Ind.: University of Notre Dame Press, 1986), vii.

6. Critics sometimes suggest that Catholic positions against birth control and abortion serve primarily to populate (or overpopulate) society with Catholics. These critics do not take into account, as Susan Nicholson points out, "the superior position accorded virginity in Catholic doctrine" (Nicholson, *Abortion and the Roman Catholic Church*, 3). That is, large Catholic families are not the only way for Catholics to live faithfully; indeed, in a history filled with asceticism and monastic celibacy, those who reproduce abundantly do not occupy the highest level of spiritual status. It is my belief that the large Catholic family reflects, not moral or spiritual loftiness, but the uniquely Catholic understandings of God and God's creation.

7. U.S. Bishops Meeting, "Resolution on Abortion," *Origins*, 16 November 1989, 395.

8. Richard Neuhaus, *The Catholic Moment: The Paradox of the Church in the Postmodern World* (Cambridge: Harper and Row, 1987), 237.

9. The encyclical responded directly to the issue of abortion only in the following passage: "It is not licit, even for the gravest reasons, to do evil so that good may follow therefrom; that is, to make into the object of a positive act of will something which is intrinsically disordered, and hence unworthy of the human person, even when the intention is to safeguard or promote individual, family or social well-being" ("Humanae Vitae: On the Regulation of Birth" [July 25, 1968], in *The Gospel of Peace and Social Justice: Catholic Social Teaching Since Pope*

John, ed. Joseph Gremillion [Maryknoll, N.Y.: Orbis Books, 1976], 434).

10. Maureen Fiedler, "Dissent within the U.S. Church: The Case of the Vatican '24,'" in *Church Polity and American Politics: Issues in Contemporary American Catholicism,* ed. Mary C. Segers (New York: Garland Press, 1990), 306.

11. It should be noted that the debate between double effect and proportionalism takes place primarily among moral theologians. While the mandates and writings of moral theology indirectly control the behavior of many American Catholics, few nonacademic Catholics have access to the philosophical parameters of this debate.

12. I believe that these debates are influenced by shifts in the reproductive practices of many American Catholics, although most of the writings associated with the debate present the arguments as if the issues were completely detached from any cultural context. For an argument which acknowledges the role of culture in the development of moral theology in general, see John Gallagher, *Time Past, Time Future: An Historical Study of Catholic Moral Theology* (New York: Paulist Press, 1990). Gallagher's is the only work to date which notes the importance of the American context in the development of proportionalist reasoning.

13. Charles E. Curran, "Absolute Norms in Medical Ethics," in *Absolutes in Moral Theology?* ed. Charles E. Curran (Washington, D.C., 1968), 113.

14. Richard McCormick, "Ambiguity in Moral Choice," in *Doing Evil to Achieve Good,* ed. Richard McCormick and Paul Ramsey (Chicago: Loyola University Press, 1978), 33.

15. Ibid., 38.

16. According to traditional Catholics, ethicists should be and are able to claim that murder, lying, and stealing, for example, are evil, without regard to the circumstances which surround any particular occurrence of these actions. Thus, for these traditionalists, some actions have an intrinsic and non-negotiable wrongness which no end can justify. Their criticism of proportionalism is precisely that it is unable to make context-free judgments regarding the morality of certain actions, and hence unable to look beyond possible "good" consequences to see the moral crime.

In response to this accusation, proportionalists employ what they believe to be the Thomistic category of premoral evil. Premoral evils are acts judged to be evil or wrong, "all other things being equal." While proportionalists argue that, in certain cases, circumstances require the performance of a premoral evil in order that a greater good be achieved, they also suggest that the premoral status of the action must be considered. As Lisa Cahill affirms, "It is always wrong to cause a [pre]moral evil for a frivolous or inadequate reason. A [pre]moral evil (death, pain, error) perpetrated disproportionately is a sin" "Teleology, Utilitarianism, and Christian Ethics," *Theological Studies* 42 [December 1981]: 611). For example, because abortion is considered a premoral evil, if it is performed for its own sake with no extenuating circumstances, it is considered by proportionalists as unjustified taking of life and therefore morally wrong. Only when the good consequences of a particular abortion compensate for the premoral evil involved can it be understood as morally acceptable. Thus, in moral evaluation, proportionalists believe that they are able both to consider the consequences of concrete action and to make abstract moral judgments.

17. Other opponents claim that proportional reasoning offers no common standard of comparison for evaluating the two or more outcomes of a given situation. One of the most forceful articulations of this position comes from Protestant ethicist Paul Ramsey, who argues that certain goods are incommensurable with one another, and therefore we have no possibility of choosing between them. "[I]f any human goods and evils are incommensurate," Ramsey claims, "then there is a genuine and irreducible ambiguity in moral choice. One cannot cut the Gordion knot by any calculus, however broad or deep or long-run; nor should he undertake to do so" (Ramsey and McCormick, *Doing Evil to Achieve Good,* 79). Ramsey offers the example of military defense of an abstract notion such as nationhood, arguing that we cannot make this choice based on proportion because we cannot compare "lives lost with the value of nationhood" (224). We can only make such a decision, Ramsey thinks, based on what we believe is right and wrong.

McCormick argues, to the contrary, that such understanding of right and wrong is itself based precisely on proportionate reasoning. Although decisions between incommensurate goods are often difficult, they are possible. As he puts the question to Ramsey, "If one cannot somehow overcome [the] indeterminacy [associated with incommensurability], on what basis could a nation ever go to war with moral uprightness?" McCormick continues, "in daily life we manage satisfactorily enough to reach decisions that involve weighing, balancing, and comparing many a rather incomparable quality in the experience of good hoped for. We manage to arrive at greater good and lesser evil verdicts in many a decision we could not quantify or demonstrate numerically. In most decisions we are comparing what seem to be overlapping species of good or alternative ways of satisfying a single need or passion, but still not goods that fit exactly at points in a single scale so that an ideal mathematician could infallibly tell us what is right" (225).

18. Proportionalism, in this critique, lacks a means for judging intrinsic value and will automatically revert to decision making based on "the greatest good for the greatest number." Lisa Cahill, a persuasive proponent of proportionalism, offers an argument to the contrary. She believes that "McCormick's recent work as a whole represents a serious move in Catholic moral thought to define a teleological position which evaluates consequences but is not utilitarian" ("Teleology, Utilitarianism, and Christian Ethics," 624). Cahill argues that the proportionalist position is teleological not only in the sense that it "hold[s] that the rightness or wrongness of an action is always determined by its tendency to produce certain consequences which are intrinsically good or bad" (603) but in the Aristotelian sense of teleology as well, that "[t]o act morally is to act for the end of realizing human excellence or virtue, the human telos" (604). Whether or not the end of an action is considered good or bad will be determined by how it relates to the teleological vision. Cahill forcefully argues that reliance upon this type of teleology sets proportionalism apart from utilitarianism.

As she suggests, "The primary difference between the utilitarianism of Bentham and Mill and the broad teleology of Aristotle, Aquinas and McCormick is that the 'good' (telos) to be sought is perceived differently" (627). For Cahill, an avowed Christian, that telos necessarily entails theological assertions. In Christian frameworks, the end of each human life as well as the end of time for humanity are formulated as a return to God. Thus, the value of an act, according to Cahill, is determined not by the distribution of human goods but rather by whether it brings us closer to God and closer to our eschatological vision. As she concludes, "the telos to be pursued is not to be understood most basically as material or finite, but rather as unlimited. In religious teleologies this telos is not only ultimately non-quantifiable but also transcendent, since it is identified with God, or union of persons in God as the 'universal common good'" (629). McCormick himself is not forthcoming regarding these matters.

19. Paul Crowley, ed., *Proceedings of the Forty-Sixth Annual Convention of the Catholic Theological Society of America*, Atlanta, 12–15 June 1991, 160. In this document, Spohn also perceptively notes that the rift between traditionalists and proportionalists was related to their respective training. As he claims, "Younger moral theologians who were trained in universities rather than seminaries have a different relation to the tradition. One commentator thought that [younger theologians] had more concern with accountability to the academy than to the church." In my estimation, both Spohn and the nameless commentator are right. The rift is indeed related to training, and the code of convictions that hold the university-trained theologians is very often produced by liberal presuppositions.

20. The moral distinction between killing and allowing someone to die has been debated in the long history of Roman Catholic moral reasoning as well as in the emergent field of medical ethics. For positions which support the moral relevance of the distinction, see Phillip Devine, *The Ethics of Homicide* (Notre Dame, Ind.: University of Notre Dame Press, 1979), 129. For positions which contest this distinction, see Nicholson, *Abortion and the Roman Catholic Church*, 72.

21. As cited in Mary C. Segers, "The Loyal Opposition: Catholics for a Free Choice," in *The Catholic Church and the Politics of Abortion*, ed. Timothy Byrnes and Mary Segers (Boulder: Westview Press, 1992), 182.

22. Kristin Luker, *Abortion and the Politics of Motherhood*, (Berkeley: University of California Press, 1984), 210. Indeed, Luker's estimate of the percentage of Catholics who receive an abortion is conservative. According to the Alan Guttmacher Institute, for example, Catholics are 30 percent more likely than Protestants to have abortions (cited by

Barbara Ferraro and Patricia Hussey, *No Turning Back: Two Nuns' Battle with the Vatican over Women's Right to Choose* [New York: Poseidon Press, 1990], 252).

23. I use American Catholicism here and in the remainder of this chapter to refer to Catholics who have "assimilated" into the American life. They stand in contradistinction to "traditional Catholics." Although the difference between these two groups can be, at times, unclear, my argument is that abortion and reproductive patterns help to delineate the boundary between them.

24. It is not the case, of course, that American Catholics only began using birth control in the last two decades. Indeed, a significant number of Catholics, in their desire to assimilate into the American middle class of the 1950s, began using various forms of birth control and even abortion in order to improve their class position. What made these contraceptive acts different from those of the American Catholics of the 1990s is that the earlier generations expressed a sense of guilt about their practices; indeed, in some instances that guilt caused them to break their relationship with the church. In the cultural milieu of American Catholicism today, however, proportionalism at once rationalizes and reflects the changes made in the lives of many American Catholics; these changes have made it possible for a person to use birth control or have an abortion and still understand themselves as being in good standing with "the church."

Whether such a person *is* in good standing with "the church" depends, of course, on how one defines the church. According to the magisterium and other officials in Rome, people practicing abortion and birth control are in the state of sin. According to American moral theologians like McCormick and Curran, precedent exists within the church's history for the methodology of proportionalism, and therefore people who use birth control and abortion are, in certain circumstances, within the circle of traditional Catholicism. This conflict is related to a struggle over who gets to define what constitutes church membership.

25. This strand of analysis originates with the thinking of John Courtney Murray. For Murray's central work, see *We Hold These Truths* (New York: Sheed and Ward, 1960). Most commentaries on the history of Catholi-

cism in America renarrate Murray's premises. See, for example, John Tracy Ellis, *American Catholicism* (Chicago: University of Chicago Press, 1970); William Halsey, *The Survival of American Innocence* (Notre Dame, Ind.: University of Notre Dame Press, 1980); David O'Brien, *Public Catholicism* (New York: Macmillan, 1989).

26. Jay P. Dolan, *The American Catholic Experience: A History from Colonial Times to the Present* (New York: Doubleday, 1985), 294.

27. Ibid., 453.

28. This free-market model could also be extended to an investigation of American attitudes toward worship. Many Americans today "shop" for churches until they find one that is in keeping with their personal tastes. Denominational affiliation is thus becoming, in many segments of the American population, a superfluous consideration. Consequently, many contemporary Catholic churches feel that they must "compete," like Protestant churches, for membership. Worship, like moral methodology, has become subject to a market economy.

29. Albert Jonsen and Stephen Toulmin, *The Abuse of Casuistry: A History of Moral Reasoning* (Berkeley: University of California Press, 1988), 2.

30. Ibid., 257. Casuistry is not, according to Jonsen and Toulmin, a new alternative, but rather one that the church has been practicing all along. In fact, James Keenan argues that the principle of double effect is itself a form of casuistry, because it acts as a summary of the practical wisdom acquired on issues involving questions of intent. That is, Keenan argues that the principle of double effect doesn't itself have a justifying function, but rather serves as a vehicle to move the analysis in keeping with similar precedent cases. Although I am persuaded by Keenan's argument, most scholars use and understand the principle not in a casuistrical register, but rather as the sole means of justification. Keenan grants this point and argues that using the principle as justification is not in keeping with historical usage. See James F. Keenan, "The Function of the Principle of Double Effect," *Theological Studies* 54, no. 2, (June 1993).

31. Jonsen and Toulmin, *The Abuse of Casuistry,* 314.

32. Ibid., 13.

33. Ibid., 136.

34. Ibid., 97, 255.
35. G. E. M. Anscombe, *Ethics, Religion, and Politics,* (Minneapolis: University of Minnesota Press, 1981), 36.
36. Other critics have made the point that Jonsen and Toulmin fail to account for the incommensurability that exists between competing moral communities. Bernard Williams, for example, writes that "[t]he trouble with casuistry . . . is that the repertory of substantive ethical concepts differs between cultures" (*Ethics and the Limits of Philosophy* [Cambridge: Harvard University Press, 1985], 96). Similarly, Philip Turner suggests that casuistry is bound to fail in contemporary settings as "widely shared institutional frameworks now seem to be missing or in the state of disarray" (review of *The Abuse of Casuistry,* in *Religious Studies Review* 17, no. 4 [October 1991], 304).
37. It could be argued as well that traditionalists have become more rigid and legalistic in an attempt to distinguish themselves from the emerging liberal theories.
38. Headline, *National Catholic Reporter,* 3 July 1992.

CHAPTER THREE
THE FUNCTION OF ABORTION IN THE RESCUE MOVEMENT

1. John Wauck, "Operation Rescue," *National Review* 41, no. 6 (7 April 1989): 41.
2. The term evangelical has several meanings. In its widest sense, "evangelical" can be applied to all Protestant churches since the Reformation as a result of their claim to base their theology fully on Scripture. Over time, and especially in the United States, "evangelical" has come to represent denominations that combine this biblical emphasis with some emotional or experiential response to revelation. George Marsden characterizes the evangelical impulse with the five following theological tenets: first, evangelicals typically hold to the Reformation doctrine of the final authority of Scripture. They reject the idea that any organization or governing body has the power to impose its interpretation on the individual. For them, the Bible is directly inspired by God and contains

the sole authority for Christian faith. Second, evangelicals believe that the real and historical character of God's saving work is accurately recorded in Scripture. The Bible is not a work of metaphor and instruction but attests to God's literal activity in the world. Third, evangelicals give priority to the salvific nature of Christ; eternal salvation is available only through personal trust in Christ. Fourth, evangelicals typically place great emphasis on missionary work, although the nature and shape of what constitutes a mission can shift. And fifth, evangelicals unwaveringly agree on the importance of leading a spiritually transformed existence. That is, they emphasize outward expression of inward conversion as a sign of future salvation. See George Marsden, *Understanding Fundamentalism and Evangelicalism* (Grand Rapids: Eerdman's, 1991).

Several scholars have argued that Marsden's formulation overlooks the strong reform impulse embedded in most historical formulations of evangelicalism. For example, Leonard Sweet argues that the primary characteristic of evangelicals is that they play out their religious impulses in social arenas. According to Sweet, the salvation of Christian souls is, for evangelicals, directly related to the feeding and care of bodies, and to other movements intended to improve the social conditions of life on earth. He argues that the term evangelicalism "refers not so much to theology as to actions bent on eradicating evil everywhere" (Leonard Sweet, *The Evangelical Tradition in America* [Macon, Ga.: Mercer University Press, 1984]). Thus, this reform impulse might also be understood as part of one definition of what it means to be evangelical; responding to the spiritual experience of revival meant, for many evangelicals, turning their religious fervor onto the sins of the world. As Sweet notes, the nineteenth-century version of this type of evangelicalism, most dramatically displayed in abolition, stemmed largely from postmillennialist beliefs about God and human nature. Nineteenth-century evangelicals believed that the kingdom of God would only be instituted on earth as humanity labored for and toward perfection. The goal of nineteenth-century evangelicalism was to continue to prepare for the kingdom of God by making the world better, a theme I will return to at the end of this chapter.

3. Paul deParrie, *The Rescuers* (Brentwood, Tenn.: Wolgemuth and Hyatt Publishers, 1989), 2. Rescuers believe that this command comes directly

from Proverbs 24:11: "Rescue those who are unjustly sentenced to death; don't stand back and let them die." It should be noted, however, that all Operation Rescue materials use *The Living Bible* as their source. *The Living Bible* is not a direct translation of Greek and Hebrew Scriptures, but rather a paraphrase of those texts for modern-day use. *TLB* was translated beginning in 1954 by Kenneth Taylor, a fundamentalist who worked for Moody Press during the day and paraphrased Scripture at night. His work was marked by conservative evangelical thinking and functions as a primary text in contemporary evangelical communities. As Taylor claimed, in the preface to *TLB*, "when the [Scripture] is not clear, then the theology of the translator is his guide." More scholarly approaches to the Book of Proverbs translate the verse differently. For example, the Revised Standard Version reads, "Rescue those who are being taken away to death, hold back those who are stumbling to the slaughter."

4. *America*, 29 April 1989.

5. *Chicago Tribune*, 20 October 1991.

6. Operation Rescue must be understood as both an extension of and a reaction against the right-to-life movement in America. Although many of the initial rescuers were members of the right-to-life movement, Operation Rescue was founded because many of the more radical Christians in the increasingly secularized pro-life movement were discontent with pro-life strategies and attitudes toward direct action. Operation Rescue split away from the larger, well-organized Right-to-Life Committee (both national and local chapters), preferring instead to voice their dissent against abortion through nonviolent civil disobedience, a method that NRLC did not endorse. The rescuers intended to close "abortuaries" at any and all costs; if arrests were made in the process, it would only bring increased attention to the intensity of their convictions. As a consequence of the rescue strategy, NRLC refused to have formal contact, and even informal association, with Operation Rescue. NRLC's president claims that their "policy is to cover [and support] only legal pro-life activities." Thus, even when rescues receive national attention from all factions of the American media, NRLC refuses to acknowledge any of the events.

7. *Washington Post*, 24 November 1991.
8. George Marsden, *Religion and American Culture* (New York: Harcourt, Brace, Jovanovich, 1990), 262.
9. Quoted in the *New York Times*, 23 September 1980.
10. *Time*, 21 October 1991.
11. Quentin Schultze, "Keeping the Faith: American Evangelicals and the Media," in *American Evangelicals in the Mass Media*, ed. Quentin Schultze (Grand Rapids, Mich.: Zondervan, 1990), 36.
12. *Operation Rescue*, (Cleveland, Ohio: American Portrait Films), VHS.
13. Connie Paige, *The Right to Lifers: Who They Are, How They Operate, and Where They Get Their Money* (New York: Summit Books, 1983), 177.
14. Robert Wuthnow, "Religion and Television: The Public and the Private," in Schultze, *American Evangelicals in the Mass Media*, 203.
15. William McLoughlin, "The Illusions and Dangers of the New Christian Right," *Foundations* 25 (April–June 1982): 128–43.
16. Grant Wacker, "Searching for Norman Rockwell: Popular Evangelicalism in Contemporary America," in Sweet, *The Evangelical Tradition in America*, 296.
17. *Time*, 21 August 1991, 28.
18. *Hotline*, 26 August 1991.
19. Grant Wacker, "Searching for Norman Rockwell," 295.
20. Paige, *The Right to Lifers*, 68.
21. Ibid., 69.

CHAPTER FOUR

CONFLICTED OVER MEN, WOMEN, AND SEX

1. The sole exception to this formula is the loosely organized movement called Pro-Life Feminism or Feminists for Life. Stemming largely from networks of communication established by factions of the pro-life movement (such as the National Right-to Life Committee, Birthright, and various Christian anti-abortion organizations), Feminists for Life argue that women should resist the oppression that men inflict upon women by resisting legalized abortion. As one pro-life feminist states,

"When abortion is available to all women, all male responsibility for fertility control has been removed. A man need only offer a woman money for the abortion and that's it: no responsibility, no relationship, no commitment. And there we are . . . recycled and used again! What we need now is a race of *women* who will stand up and say NO! The violence ends here. The misogyny ends here. The destruction of our children ends here. No longer will our bodies be used to write messages of fear and hatred. We hold within our bodies the power of creation, the power to nourish and sustain life. We shall not pervert these powers to death" (Cecilia Voss Koch, "Reflecting as FFL Celebrates Its Tenth Birthday," in *Pro-Life Feminism,* ed. Gail Grenier Sweet [Toronto: Life Cycle Books, 1985], 23; this collection operates as the central text of the Feminists for Life organization).

2. For a more detailed account of the Physician's Crusade, see James Mohr, *Abortion in America* (New York: Oxford University Press, 1978).

3. Ninia Baehr, *Abortion without Apology: A Radical History for the 1990's* (Boston: South End Press, 1990), 3.

4. Between 1967 and the legalization of abortion in 1973, only fourteen states had passed legislation permitting medical abortions which fell loosely within ALI recommendations. Even with these bills, however, state laws varied greatly. One reporter recounts the following discrepancies: "Between 1970 and 1973 abortion was legal in New York, prohibited in New Hampshire, legal in Mississippi if the pregnant woman's life was in danger or she had been raped. You could get a legal abortion in Alaska if you could prove you lived there. You could get a legal abortion in Georgia if your mental health was in grave danger, or if you had been raped, but not if you had become pregnant through incest; in California you could get a legal abortion if you had become pregnant through incest, but not if you said you wanted an abortion because the fetus was deformed" (Cynthia Gorney, "Abortion, Once Upon a Time in America," *Washington Post,* 26 April 1989.

5. See especially accounts of various doctors in Patricia Miller, *The Worst of Times* (New York: HarperCollins), 1993.

6. Birth control pills are regulated by medical prescription. Getting the pill requires an appointment with a doctor who can write the prescription.

While such doctors often work in free clinics, women must be able to get to the clinic and also must be able to afford the product once the prescription is written.

7. The 1980s and 1990s saw the publication of many collections devoted to the issue of illegal abortion in the pre-*Roe* era. The story these works recount is complicated. On the one hand, their primary intent is to explicitly portray the horrors associated with unsafe abortion; thus, they are so filled with images of blood and death that the reader is persuaded that only physicians in hospitals should perform abortions, and that abortion should remain legal so that safety can be ensured. On the other hand, many of these works simultaneously suggest a competing story, that throughout history, women have always sought illegal *but safe* abortions from nonmedical providers such as midwives and through non-medically authorized techniques such as menstrual extraction. The second story tells us that abortion is a natural part of history, as long as it resides within the power of women, not within medicine. These competing narratives are recorded in the following works: Miller, *The Worst of Times;* Ellen Messer and Kathryn May, *Back Rooms: An Oral History of the Illegal Abortion Movement* (New York: Simon and Schuster), 1988; Angela Bonavoglia, ed., *The Choices We Made* (New York: Random House), 1991; Rita Townsend and Ann Perkins, *Bitter Fruit: Women's Experiences of Unplanned Pregnancy, Abortion, and Adoption* (Alameda, Calif.: Hunter House), 1991; Linda Bird Francke, *The Ambivalence of Abortion* (New York: Random House), 1978; Rebecca Chalker and Carol Downer, *A Woman's Book of Choices: Abortion, Menstrual Extraction, RU-486* (New York: Four Walls, Eight Windows), 1992. It is precisely this paradox which spawned feminists in the pre-*Roe* era not only to fight for changes in abortion legislation, but also to develop alternative networks for abortion such as JANE (see below). In the wake of the increasingly restrictive abortion legislation of the past decade, several current feminist organizations are again attempting to establish alternative "illegal" networks to be used if abortion rights falter.

8. The term "radical" was initially used pejoratively by commentators who opposed this feminist agenda. Feminists took on the name for themselves, and the meaning of the term shifted into a more positive light.

NOTES TO PAGES 63–67

However, although these women were self-proclaimed "radical feminists," I will avoid using this terminology in the remainder of this chapter. The term "radical feminist" has been employed by different groups with different ideologies at different times. Most recently it has been used in typographies of feminism to refer to a category similar to the "essentialist feminists" I discuss below, a group which stands in stark ideological opposition to earlier, pro-abortion feminists. For use of the term "radical" to signify later competing movements, see Allison Jaggar, *Feminist Politics and Human Nature* (Sussex: Harvester Press, 1983), 83–122 and 249–302. See also Rosemarie Tong, *Feminist Thought: A Comprehensive Introduction* (Boulder: Westview Press, 1989), 71–138. In general, "radical" usually implies that adherents believe that the ideology and strategies of their particular group will ultimately lead to revolution and reconstruction. The varying plans for these upheavals, as we shall see, are in fact very different.

9. Robin Morgan, "The Women's Revolution," introduction to *Sisterhood is Powerful*, ed. Robin Morgan (New York: Random House, 1970), xx.

10. For a detailed account of the associations between the New Left and women's liberation, see Sara Evans, *Personal Politics: The Roots of Women's Liberation in the Civil Rights Movement and the New Left* (New York: Vintage Books, 1979).

11. Baehr, *Abortion without Apology*, 33.

12. Ellen Willis, foreword to *Daring to be Bad: Radical Feminism in America, 1967–1975*, by Alice Echols (Minneapolis: University of Minnesota Press, 1989), viii.

13. Baehr, *Abortion without Apology*, 30.

14. For a first-hand account of a doctor who performed such abortions, see Bernard Nathanson, *Aborting America* (New York: Pinnacle Books), 1981. It should be noted that Dr. Nathanson has since changed his position on abortion and is in fact one of the leaders of the pro-life movement (and the host of the anti-abortion film *The Silent Scream*). His narrative is nevertheless useful here as it clearly demonstrates the haphazardness with which illegal abortions were obtained.

15. The organization was called JANE because each member concealed her

everyday identity by referring to herself and the other twenty-odd women in the organization as "Jane." For more information, see "Just Call 'Jane,'" in *From Abortion to Reproductive Freedom: Transforming a Movement,* ed. Marlene Gerber Fried, (Boston: South End Press, 1990), 93–100, and Pauline Bart, "Seizing the Means of Reproduction: An Illegal Feminist Abortion Collective—How and Why it Worked," *Qualitative Sociology* 10, no. 4, (winter 1987): 339–57.

16. Quoted in Pauline B. Bart and Melinda Bart Schlesinger, "Collective Work and Self-Identity: The Effect of Working in a Feminist Illegal Abortion Collective," in *Workplace Democracy and Social Change,* ed. Frank Lindenfeld and Joyce Rothchild Whitt (Boston: Porter-Sargent, 1981), 139–53.

17. It should be noted that Carol Downer, the progenitor of this technique and organizer of the movement, does not identify this as an abortion. According to her, the procedure should be performed monthly to avoid cramps, bleeding, and other menstrual discomforts. Abortion can only happen, according to Downer, if a pregnancy confirmed by tests is known to exist. Since these women extract their menses monthly and are discouraged from using pregnancy tests, no one involved can be certain when an abortion has actually been performed. See Chalker and Downer, *A Woman's Book of Choices.*

18. Rosalyn Baxandall, *Women and Abortion: The Body as Battleground,* Open Magazine Pamphlet Series, pamphlet 17 (Westfield, N.J.: Open Media, 1992), 12.

19. For a secondary account of this ideology, see Echols, *Daring to be Bad.*

20. I have had difficulty finding a neutral descriptive name for this second tendency of feminism. In many current typologies, it is referred to as "radical feminism"—a misleading term as it has also been used to describe the first stage. See note 8 above. Opponents such as Ellen Willis refer to this strand as "neo-Victorian" feminism *(No More Nice Girls* [Middletown, Conn.: Wesleyan University Press, 1992], 29–30). Other conversations identify it as "essentialist feminism," arguing that its proponents believe that the differences between men and women are ontological or biologically essential. In her comprehensive history of

contemporary feminism, Alice Echols refers to it as "cultural feminism."
I am equally uncomfortable with this term because I believe that all
feminisms are cultural.

21. Adrienne Rich, *Of Woman Born* (New York: Norton, 1976), 31–32.
22. Andrea Dworkin, *Right-Wing Women* (New York: Perigee Books, 1978),
83.
23. As quoted in Echols, *Daring to Be Bad,* 211.
24. Ibid., 5.
25. Ibid., 9.
26. Echols is of course not alone in her evaluation of this type of feminism.
For a strong critique of "cultural feminism," see Brooke, "The Retreat to
Cultural Feminism" in *Feminist Revolution,* ed. Redstockings (New
York: Random House, 1975), 79–84. For an interesting critique of a particular kind of second-stage formulation (that of Betty Friedan's later
writings and the work of Jean Bethke Elshtain), see Judith Stacey, "The
New Conservative Feminism," *Feminist Studies* 9, no. 3 (fall 1983).
27. Echols, *Daring to Be Bad,* 240.
28. Ibid., 5.
29. Catherine MacKinnon, *Feminism Unmodified* (Cambridge: Harvard
University Press, 1987), 97.
30. Precisely when and how the "pro-choice" movement began is contested.
For feminists involved in the first pro-abortion campaign, the rhetoric
of pro-choice was itself a recognition of and concession to the opposition "pro-life." See Baxandall, Women and Abortion. Self-described
members of pro-choice, however, often trace their roots back to the
1960s and see little or no disjunction between reform and repeal. For
example, Suzanne Staggenborg traces the pro-choice movement back to
the first stage of feminism but claims that the movement didn't become
well organized or powerful until after 1973 (*The Pro-Choice Movement:
Organization and Activism in the Abortion Conflict* [New York: Oxford
University Press, 1991], 3). Indeed, the larger point of Staggenborg's
work argues that social change comes both from within institutionalized settings (such as medicine and law), and from outside, at grassroots
levels. She is able to make this claim, I suggest, by lumping the first stage
of feminism together with the pro-choice movement, the former serving

as her example of grassroots, confrontational change, the latter providing the institutionalized means. From my viewpoint, this collapse is worrisome not only because most women of the first stage explicitly deny the association, but also because the two ideologies function entirely differently.

31. In some cases, the "single issue" at stake is formulated as the conviction to "keep abortion both safe and legal." However, NARAL—one of the major single-issue abortion organizations—decided to forgo the safety aspect in order to focus fully on legality. As one NARAL activist stated, "There were other groups formed to keep abortion safe, and we decided to exclude that word from our mission statement. That's not part of our mission to keep it safe" (quoted in Staggenborg, *The Pro-Choice Movement*, 107). Thus, in the ideology of single-issue organizing, the more narrowly the issue is configured, the more support it will get.

32. As quoted in Flora Davis, *Moving the Mountain: The Women's Movement in America since 1960* (New York: Touchstone Books, 1991), 142.

33. For an exhaustive review of the strategies surrounding the single issue of ERA, see Donald Mathews and Jane Sherron DeHart, *Sex, Gender, and the Politics of ERA* (New York: Oxford University Press, 1990).

34. Although neither of these groups had been involved in the abortion issue before 1973, both became heavily involved in pro-choice lobbying after 1973. By 1973, all factions of the National Organization for Women had also formally aligned themselves with pro-choice politics.

35. Staggenborg, *The Pro-Choice Movement*, 42.

36. Ibid., 31

37. Ibid., 87.

CHAPTER FIVE

THE UNEASY MARRIAGE BETWEEN FEMINISM AND "PRO-CHOICE"

1. Sterilization came to the forefront of human rights concerns in the mid 1970s when feminists discovered that many poor and minority women were coerced into being sterilized. In some cases, women were routinely sterilized during an abortion procedure, without their consent or knowledge. These sterilizations were a blatantly racist attempt to limit

"undesirable" populations. For further accounts of racial sterilization abuse, see Angela Davis, "Racism, Birth Control, and Reproductive Rights," in *From Abortion to Reproductive Freedom: Transforming a Movement,* ed. Marlene Gerber Fried (Boston: South End Press, 1990), 15–27.

2. As quoted in Suzanne Staggenborg, *The Pro-Choice Movement: Organization and Activism in the Abortion Conflict* (New York: Oxford University Press, 1991), 110.

3. Rosalyn Baxandall, *Women and Abortion: The Body as Battleground,* Open Magazine Pamphlet Series, pamphlet 17 (Westfield, N.J.: Open Media, 1992), 10.

4. Marlene Gerber Fried, "Transforming the Reproductive Rights Movement: The Post-Webster Agenda," in *From Abortion to Reproductive Freedom,* 6.

5. It is important to state clearly that the reproductive rights activists were not at all opposed to legalized abortion; rather, they simply felt that such an agenda was not enough. As Rosalind Petchesky states it, "we have to adopt a two-pronged strategy for the movement: first, a defensive legislative strategy that attempts to secure abortion rights, and second, an aggressive electoral and public education (including media) campaign that clearly and creatively embeds abortion in a much wider set of issues that affect poor, and young women of color" ("Change Strategies, Change Vision," in *New Directions for Women* 18, no. 5, [September/October 1989]: 1).

6. Rhonda Copeland, "From Privacy to Autonomy: The Conditions for Sexual and Reproductive Freedom," in Fried, *From Abortion to Reproductive Freedom,* 33.

7. Marlene Gerber Fried, "Transforming the Reproductive Rights Movement: The Post-Webster Agenda," in ibid., 8.

8. See Beverly Smith, "Choosing Ourselves: Black Women and Abortion," 83–87, and Angela Davis, "Racism, Birth Control, and Reproductive Rights," 15–27, both in ibid.

9. Rosalind Petchesky, *Abortion and Women's Choice: The State, Sexuality, and Reproductive Freedom* (Boston: Northeastern University Press, 1984), 25.

10. Ibid., 25.

11. Ibid., 13.
12. Ibid., 67.
13. Ibid., 89.
14. As Petchesky analyzes *Roe*, "the changes that occurred during the 1960's and 1970's [are not located] within a framework of expounded 'individual choices' or individual achievement, but within a new range of social conditions that redefine the terms of 'normal life' for women, [that is,] capitalism required reliable means of fertility control to support a growing demand for female labor power" (ibid., 115).
15. Ibid., 13.
16. Ibid., 3.
17. "In the long run, the kind of grass-roots organizing carried out with the aid of professional leaders in organizations like NARAL and NOW may be more enduring than the grass-roots participation engendered by the decentralized and informal structure of an organization like R2N2" (Staggenborg, *The Pro-Choice Movement*, 122).
18. For an excellent portrayal of the systemtic nature of female poverty in America, see Valerie Polakow, *Lives on the Edge: Single Mothers and Their Children in the Other America* (Chicago: University of Chicago Press, 1993). Polakow demonstrates how many women's lives are destroyed in the attempt to care and provide a life for their children, and in so doing makes it clear that many women do not have the ability to choose to have the baby.
19. As I explained in chapter 1, in using the term "liberal" here, I do not refer to "open-mindedness," but rather to the set of ideas that arose during the Enlightenment which placed primary value on the autonomous individual. These philosophical developments accompanied the western European movement to end religious warfare by relocating the political power of the kings and bishops in the realm of the "citizen." Thus, it should be remembered that although things like individual value, equality, autonomy, and fairness for all might seem self-evident to our late-twentieth-century moral sensibilities, they are in fact historical developments which arose in response to concrete historical oppressions.
20. Zillah Eisenstein, *The Radical Future of Liberal Feminism* (Boston: Northeastern University Press, 1981), 5. It should be noted that Eisen-

stein, along with Susan Wendell, argues that liberal feminism in fact transcends the shortcomings of liberal theory. Wendell, for example, maintains that because of its commitments to women's issues, liberal feminism is free of the problems associated with "abstract individualism, certain kinds of individualistic approaches to morality and society, valuing the mental/rational over the physical/emotional, and the traditional liberal way of drawing the line between the public and the private" ("A [Qualified] Defense of Liberal Feminism," *Hypatia* 2, no. 2 [summer 1987]: 66). While I am certainly sympathetic to this idea, I am unpersuaded that it is an accurate description of pro-choice politics, for which the precepts of liberal subjectivity (to which Wendell opposes liberal feminism) serve as a foundation.

21. Michael Warner, "The Mass Public and the Mass Subject," in *Habermas and the Public Sphere,* ed. Craig Calhoun (Cambridge: MIT Press, 1992), 382, 384.

22. The liberal, capitalist workplace also cannot provide the necessary extra support for raising children. In today's ideology, we believe a person ought to be rewarded for the work that he or she does, independent of particular needs. If two people are performing the same tasks at a job, one ought not be paid more—we believe—because he has children. Indeed, our liberal mentality often allows women to be paid less precisely because they are the ones who have children and are therefore thought to be less dependable.

23. For more information on the historical development of separate spheres, see Nancy Cott, *The Bonds of Womanhood: "Woman's Sphere" in New England* (New Haven: Yale University Press, 1977); Barbara Epstein, *The Politics of Domesticity: Women, Evangelism, and Temperance in Nineteenth-Century America* (Middletown, Conn.: Wesleyan University Press, 1981); Ann Douglas, *The Feminization of American Culture* (New York: Doubleday, 1988); Mary Ryan, *Cradle of the Middle Class: The Family in Oneida County, New York, 1790–1865* (Cambridge: Cambridge University Press, 1981); Nancy Hewitt, *Women's Activism and Social Change: Rochester, New York, 1822–1872* (Ithaca: Cornell University Press, 1984).

24. In liberal theory, parents instill the values in their children that are

meant to ensure justice in the home. It is precisely these emotions which the individual later uses to understand fairness in the public realm. The family is, however, exempt from the justice guaranteed in the public sphere precisely because it is "private." Thus, in liberal theory, the family does the work of moral training but reaps none of the benefits or protections of liberal society. For extended analysis, see Susan Moller Okin, *Justice, Gender, and the Family* (New York: Basic Books, 1989).

25. See, for example, Ann Jones, *Next Time She'll Be Dead: Battering and How to Stop It* (Boston: Beacon Press, 1994).

26. Katharine Bartlett and Roseanne Kennedy, eds., *Feminist Legal Theory: Readings in Law and Gender* (Boulder: Westview Press, 1991), 3.

27. Wendy Williams, "The Equality Crisis: Some Reflections on Culture, Courts, and Feminism," in Bartlett and Kennedy, *Feminist Legal Theory,* 22.

28. In *Making All the Difference: Inclusion, Exclusion, and American Law* (Ithaca: Cornell University Press, 1990), Martha Minow rightly identifies the central problem here as what she calls "men as norm." Minow attempts to reconceptualize a way of using rights language that is divorced from the autonomous male subject. She does this by locating the norm within the entire community. While I support such a reconstruction, I am less sanguine about the possibilities of integrating these particular philosophical advances into everyday practices.

29. Owen Flanagan and Kathryn Jackson, "Justice, Care, and Gender: The Kohlberg-Gilligan Debate Revisited," in *An Ethic of Care: Feminist and Interdisciplinary Perspectives,* ed. Mary Jeanne Larrabee (New York: Routledge, 1993), 71.

30. Carol Gilligan, *In a Different Voice: Psychological Theory and Women's Development* (Cambridge: Harvard University Press, 1982), 26.

31. Ibid., 28

32. Ibid., 28, 29. For a clear and cogent description of caring as an activity, see Joan Tronto, *Moral Boundaries: A Political Argument for an Ethic of Care* (New York: Routledge, 1993), 79.

33. Although there has been a significant amount of controversy surrounding Gilligan's work, many theorists have advocated a combination of both ethical strands. See Charlotte Bunch, "A Global Perspective on

Feminist Ethics and Diversity," and Elizabeth Bartlett, "Beyond Either/
Or," in *Explorations in Feminist Ethics: Theory and Practice,* ed. Eve
Browning Cole and Susan Coultrap-McQuin (Bloomington: Indiana
University Press, 1992); Annette Baier, "The Need for More than Jus-
tice," in *Science, Morality, and Feminist Theory,* ed. Marsha Hanen and
Kai Nielsen (Calgary: University of Calgary Press, 1987), 47.

34. Elizabeth Schneider, "The Dialectic of Rights and Politics: Perspectives
from the Women's Movement," in *Women, the State, and Welfare,* ed.
Linda Gordon (Madison: University of Wisconsin Press, 1990), 235.

35. The discussions that surfaced as a result of *In a Different Voice* are complex and take on issues which are beyond the scope of this chapter. For
critiques, evaluations, and reformulations of Gilligan's premises from
philosophical perspectives, see Eve Browning Cole and Susan Coultrap-
McQuin, *Explorations in Feminist Ethics;* Claudia Card, ed., *Feminist
Ethics* (Lawrence: University of Kansas Press, 1991); and Eva Feder Kittay
and Diana T. Meyers, *Women and Moral Theory* (Totowa, N.J.: Row-
man and Littlefield, 1987). For a more psychologically based evaluation
of Gilligan's theory, see Mary Jeanne Larrabee, *An Ethic of Care.* For a
collection which traces the history of these caring tendencies in women's
writings on ethics, see Elizabeth Frazer, Jennifer Hornsby, and Sabina
Lovibond, eds., *Ethics: A Feminist Reader* (Cambridge: Basil Blackwell,
1992).

36. See Sara Ruddick, *Maternal Thinking: Toward a Politics of Peace* (Boston:
Beacon Press, 1989); Nel Noddings, *Caring: A Feminine Approach to
Ethics and Moral Education* (Berkeley: University of California Press,
1984).

37. See Susan Faludi, *Backlash: The Undeclared War against American Women*
(New York: Crown, 1991), and Katha Pollitt, "Are Women Morally
Superior to Men?" *The Nation,* 28 December 1992, 799–807.

38. See Joan Tronto, "Beyond Gender Difference to a Theory of Care,"
Signs: Journal of Women and Culture in Society 12: 644–63.

39. Seyla Benhabib, "The Generalized and the Concrete Other," in *Feminism as Critique,* ed. Seyla Benhabib and Drucilla Cornell (Minneapolis:
University of Minnesota Press, 1987), 77–96. For a more extensive
critique of these points, see also Seyla Benhabib, *Situating the Self: Gen-*

der, Community, and Postmodernism in Contemporary Ethics (New York: Routledge, 1992).

40. Ibid., 87.

41. This is not a claim that abstract, universal principles exist. Rather, it is a claim that in every context, community, or narrative, ideas exist about what the good is or could be. Between different narratives or communities, conflicts over principles can and do exist. (Indeed, this book maps these conflicts on the issue of abortion.)

42. Often this act of paying attention to context can be viewed as empathetic, nurturing, or "caring" about those around us. Always it means that the rightness or wrongness of an act is not solely dependent on the principles at stake, but also involved with the demands of a situation. These demands can only be discovered by attending to circumstances.

43. If justice and care are central to everyone's everyday life, we escape the problem whereby a certain group of people become primarily caregivers and are eventually thought to be undeserving of equality and justice. Care should not be something that is available only in the domestic sphere; rather, in the moral and political actions that constitute daily life, connection, context, and relationship should be central. Simultaneously, it is not the case that justice is only available in the public sphere; principles of fairness and equality are essential to close and intimate relationships as well. In understanding that justice and care are interdependent, we can also reconstruct workplaces as sites of collaboration rather than competition.

44. Tronto, *Moral Boundaries*, 161.

45. Fried, "Transforming the Reproductive Rights Movement," 8.

CHAPTER SIX

CHRISTIANITY AND THE ABORTION WARS

1. Albert Jonsen and Stephen Toulmin, *The Abuse of Casuistry: A History of Moral Reasoning* (Berkeley: University of California Press, 1988), 257.

2. Pierre J. Payer, *Sex and the Penitentials: The Development of a Sexual Code, 550–1150* (Toronto: University of Toronto Press, 1984), 7.

3. John McNeill and Helen Gamer, *Medieval Handbooks of Penance* (New York: Columbia University Press, 1938), 9.

4. Jonsen and Toulmin, *The Abuse of Casuistry,* 99.

5. "Penitential of Bede," reprinted in McNeill and Gamer, *Medieval Handbooks of Penance,* 223.

6. *Institutionum* I. 18. 43–44, as quoted in Jonsen and Toulmin, *The Abuse of Casuistry,* 259.

7. Jonsen and Toulmin, *The Abuse of Casuistry,* 255.

8. Lawrence Blum, "Gilligan and Kohlberg: Implications for Moral Theory," *Ethics* 98: 474.

9. Ibid., 475.

10. In some instances, it won't be so easy to get the man involved. For example, perhaps the woman doesn't know who the father is, or perhaps he doesn't go to any church and therefore may have no community willing to hold him accountable. These are difficult situations, and I can offer no foolproof remedy that will guarantee the father's involvement. I can suggest, however, that if many of our churches began to deal more realistically and effectively with situations of unwanted pregnancy, they might come to play a more vital role in the life of young people today.

11. The question arises here as to whether the church also has a stake in non-Christian babies. As I will argue more specifically in the next chapter, the primary concern of Christians ought to be the situations and realities governing Christian women with unwanted pregnancies. Only when we can successfully take care of the women and children in our own communities can we then turn outward and offer something to non-Christians. And what we will be able to offer non-Christians should we get that far is not an abstract principle about when life begins nor even a moral platitude about hospitality. We will be able to offer non-Christian women a place where they and their children will be welcomed and practices which will rejoice in them.

CHAPTER SEVEN

SUBJECTIVITY, FRAGMENTATION, AND THE LAW

1. Sue Hertz, *Caught in the Crossfire* (New York: Prentice-Hall, 1991), 156.

NOTES TO PAGES 132–136

2. Rita Townsend and Ann Perkins, *Bitter Fruit: Women's Experiences of Unplanned Pregnancy, Abortion, and Adoption* (Alameda, Calif.: Hunter House, 1991), 39.

3. Mary Poovey, "The Abortion Question and the Death of Man," *Feminists Theorize the Political*, ed. Judith Butler and Joan Scott (New York: Routledge, 1992), 242.

4. Some people negotiate only two or three communities; others live in dozens. Some people live in only one. I do not want to either prescribe or describe multiple memberships for all human beings; everybody is different. I simply want to pose multiple memberships as a theoretical possibility.

5. Iris Marion Young, *Throwing Like a Girl and Other Essays in Feminist Philosophy and Social Theory* (Bloomington: Indiana University Press, 1990), 162–63.

6. Catharine MacKinnon, "Reflections on Sex Equality under Law," *Yale Law Journal* 100 (1991): 1316.

7. In today's culture, this shift from a woman to a pregnant woman takes place either as a result of technology (for those who can afford pregnancy tests, amniocentesis, CVS, sonography) or when the pregnancy becomes visible (when the woman "shows"). In both cases, the transition occurs as people other than the woman recognize the pregnancy. I think this is an interesting change from the nineteenth-century, where pregnancy was signified by "quickening," the moment when the woman felt the fetus move within her womb. In this earlier scenario, the woman perhaps had more control over the definition of her pregnancy.

8. Ronald Dworkin, *Life's Dominion: An Argument about Abortion, Euthanasia, and Individual Freedom* (New York: Knopf, 1993), 22.

9. Ibid., 11.

10. In Dworkin's view, even pro-lifers advocate abortion in cases of rape, incest, or to save the life of the mother, and therefore they really do not believe the fetus is a full person. Similarly, he asserts that few feminists believe that abortion is equivalent to birth control or to the decision not to conceive in the first place.

11. Ibid., 79.

12. Dworkin's position here resembles that of Engelhardt (reviewed in

chapter 1) for whom the value of life is quantitatively calculable.

13. Elizabeth Mensch and Alan Freeman, *The Politics of Virtue: Is Abortion Debatable?* (Durham: Duke University Press, 1993), 151.

14. Ibid., 151, 149.

15. It is not only feminists who would oppose these proposed compromises. Both Roman Catholics and evangelicals might object to language which posits the value of life as being intrinsic, as most would understand such value as coming directly from God.

16. Roger Rosenblatt, *Life Itself: Abortion in the American Mind* (New York: Random House, 1992), 138. For a similar formulation, see Donald Judges, *Hard Choices, Lost Voices: How the Abortion Conflict has Divided America, Distorted Constitutional Rights, and Damaged the Courts* (Chicago: Ivan Dee, 1993). Judges argues that "people on both sides of the issue share an intuitive, naturally human abhorrence of the deliberate dismemberment of what looks like a tiny human being" (287). Like Rosenblatt, he argues that although we must permit abortion in this pluralistic country, we should also discourage it.

In a less direct fashion, Laurence Tribe suggests that the Court's position articulated in *Roe* provides a compromise for conflicting groups through the terms of democracy and privacy. Tribe opposes those factions of the pro-life movement that—through confrontational style and focus on this single issue—challenge the supremacy of democracy. Tribe suggests that, as Americans, we must stand in favor of liberty for all and refuse to be bullied by "the kind of single-issue campaigning that has already distorted the face of national [politics]" (*Abortion: The Clash of Absolutes* [New York: Norton, 1990], 6). Tribe thus invests himself in keeping the state and religion separate, and in doing so he is able to grant the ideology of the state (tolerance) primacy.

17. Like Dworkin, Rosenblatt claims that as Americans, we have already learned to live together, disagreeing about abortion as we disagree about other matters. In a series of interviews conducted in Iowa—because, as he says, "Iowa has always been an especially good place for getting at the heart of what the country is thinking"—Rosenblatt discovered that this "permissive but discouraging attitude" had already been adopted by most Americans. Therefore, he asserts, it is only small groups on either

extreme (such as Catholics, evangelicals, and feminists) that constitute the abortion debate.

18. Resistance to tolerance and to the ideological split between public and private which underpins it can be seen not only in the rhetoric of many Christian ideologies, but also in many feminist constructions as well, for example, "the personal is the political."

19. Ruth Colker, *Abortion and Dialogue: Pro-Choice, Pro-Life, and American Law* (Bloomington: Indiana University Press, 1992), 85. Colker rightly notes that equality as it is currently interpreted often works to the detriment of women for precisely the same reasons I suggested in chapter 5. That is, when encumbrances such as pregnancy or childcare are not viewed as gender specific, women who have such responsibilities are treated unfairly. Corker recognizes that equality only guarantees full rights to those whose "personal choices" have left them unencumbered (88).

20. Peter Wenz, *Abortion Rights as Religious Freedom* (Philadelphia: Temple University Press, 1992), xii. Wenz's argument is a response to criticisms of *Roe* which argue against privacy in order to overturn the decision. By placing abortion rights within freedom of religion, Wenz attempts to retain a women's right to abort without the foundation of privacy.

21. Ibid., 161.

22. Ninia Baehr, *Abortion without Apology: A Radical History for the 1990's* (Boston: South End Press, 1990), 33.

23. Indeed, several theologians and Christian ethicists advocated the repeal movement that preceded *Roe*. Robert Drinan, for example, supported repeal rather than reform because reform would suggest that certain abortions were deemed morally acceptable by the state, whereas with repeal, the state simply held no position. "Under [repeal]," claimed Drinan in 1967, "the law would not be required to approve or disapprove the choices of parents and physicians as to who may be born or not born" (cited in Colin Francome, *Abortion Freedom: A Worldwide Movement* [New York: Prentice, 1984], 113).

24. The question arises here about how this model of repeal will be received by Christians involved in anti-abortion organizations such as Operation Rescue. Wouldn't repeal be a loss for them? What would prevent them

and other Christians from marshaling aggressive retaliations such as bombing clinics and shooting doctors? While my communitarian approach to abortion cannot solve the problem of violence completely, I suggest that in this model, it falls on the shoulders of all other Christians (in addition to the law) to convince those militant members of the Body of Christ to expend their energies in the service of women in their own church. In this communitarian approach, it becomes the task of enthusiastic evangelicals—as well as mainline Protestants and Roman Catholics—to display for outsiders why the Christian worldview is both exciting and desirable. With such communal checks and pressure, the drastic actions associated with abortion politics might abate. It is also worth pointing out that keeping abortion under legal regulation has not prevented such atrocious actions.

25. Mary Poovey, "The Abortion Question and the Death of Man," 252.

Index

◄○►

LIBRARY OF CONGRESS CATALOGING-IN-PUBLICATION DATA

Rudy, Kathy
    Beyond pro-life and pro-choice : moral diversity in the abortion
debate / Kathy Rudy.
        p.   cm.
    Includes bibliographical references and index.
    ISBN 0-8070-426-X
    1. Abortion—Moral and ethical aspects.   2. Abortion—Religious
aspects—Christianity.   I. Title.
HQ767.15.R83   1996
363.4'6—dc20   95-47648